LEGACY *Leadership*

Application Exercises and Journal

Implementing the 5 Best Practices and
Critical Success Skills of Legacy Leadership

Dr. Jeannine Sandstrom and Dr. Lee Smith

ISBN# 978-0-9974943-2-7

THE LEGACY LEADERSHIP APPLICATION JOURNAL. Copyright 2017-2021. CoachWorks® International, Inc., Dallas, Texas USA. All rights reserved. The Legacy Leadership® Model, Program and System was written and developed by Dr. Jeannine Sandstrom. and Dr. Lee Smith and no part of this publication may be reproduced in any form, or by any means whatsoever without written permission from the publisher, except in the case of brief quotations embodied in critical articles and reviews with appropriate acknowledgements.

CoachWorks®, Legacy Leadership®, Legacy Leader®, The Legacy Leader Company®, The Legacy Leadership® Competency Inventory (LLCI)™, LeaderShifts™, Collaborative Conversation™, Holder of Vision and Values™, Creator of Collaboration and Innovation™, Influencer of Inspiration and Leadership™, Advocator of Differences and Community™, Calibrator of Responsibility and Accountability™.

CoachWorks® Press, Dallas, TX.

If you would like further information about the Legacy Leadership® Program and other CoachWorks® services and products, please visit our website at www.CoachWorks.com (and www.LegacyLeadership.com) and contact us at info@CoachWorks.com.

This book is intended to be used with the book *"Legacy Leadership: The Leader's Guide to Greatness"* (2nd Edition, ISBN-13: 978-0997494310) but may also be used as a stand alone piece.

CoachWorks® International Corporation
Dallas, Texas USA
www.CoachWorks.com
www.LegacyLeadership.com

Table of Contents

Introduction 7
What is Legacy Leadership®? 9
   Legacy Leadership® Model 11
   The Essence 12
   Expected Outcomes 13
   Definitions 14
   The "Being" and "Doing" of Legacy Leadership 15
   Aerial Views 15
      BP 1: Holder of Vision and Values™ 16
      BP 2: Creator of Collaboration and Innovation™ 17
      BP 3: Influencer of Inspiration and Leadership™ 18
      BP 4: Advocate of Differences and Community™ 19
      BP 5: Calibrator of Responsibility and Accountability™ 20
   The Critical Success Skills (CSS) 21
   The Legacy Leadership Logo 22
   Know, Believe and Do 23
   Using This Application Workbook 24
   Initial Development Plan 25

Best Practice 1: Holder of Vision and Values™ 27
   Where Are You Now? *(Self Assessment)* 28
   Apply the Basics 30
   Drill Downs *(Critical Success Skill Exercises)* 35
      CSS1 36
      CSS2 38
      CSS3 40
      CSS4 42
      CSS5 44
      CSS6 46
      CSS7 48
      CSS8 50
      CSS9 52
      CSS10 54
   Developing Personal Vision 56
   Developing Values 58
   Corporate Values 60
   Application Notes BP1 61

Best Practice 2: Creator of Collaboration and Innovation™ 63
   Where Are You Now? *(Self Assessment)* 64
   Apply the Basics 66
   Drill Downs *(Critical Success Skill Exercises)* 71
      CSS1 72
      CSS2 74
      (continued next page)

Table of Contents (continued)

Drill Downs *(BP2 continued)*
- CSS3 76
- CSS4 78
- CSS5 80
- CSS6 82
- CSS7 84
- CSS8 86
- CSS9 88
- CSS10 90

Building Trust.. 92
Developing The Art of Asking Leadership Questions.. 94
Application Notes BP2 95

Best Practice 3: Influencer of Inspiration and Leadership™ **97**
Where Are You Now? *(Self Assessment)*... 98
Apply the Basics... 100
Drill Downs *(Critical Success Skill Exercises)* 105
- CSS1 106
- CSS2 108
- CSS3 110
- CSS4 112
- CSS5 114
- CSS6 116
- CSS7 118
- CSS8 120
- CSS9 122
- CSS10 124

The Influential Leader.. 126
Situational Story Development... 127
Application Notes BP3 133

Best Practice 4: Advocator of Differences and Community™ **135**
Where Are You Now? *(Self Assessment)*.. 136
Apply the Basics.. 138
Drill Downs *(Critical Success Skill Exercises)* 143
- CSS1 144
- CSS2 146
- CSS3 148
- CSS4 150
- CSS5 152
- CSS6 154
- CSS7 156
- CSS8 158
- CSS9 162
- CSS10 164

Personal Work 166
Application Notes BP4 169

Best Practice 5: Calibrator of Responsibility and Accountability™ **171**
Where Are You Now? *(Self Assessment)* 172
Apply the Basics 174
Drill Downs *(Critical Success Skill Exercises)* 179
    CSS1 180
    CSS2 182
    CSS3 184
    CSS4 186
    CSS5 188
    CSS6 190
    CSS7 192
    CSS8 194
    CSS9 196
    CSS10 198
Mapping the Plan for Organizational Results 200
Mapping the Plan for Professional Results 201
Application Notes BP5 202

Further Development 204

Legacy Leadership Competency Inventory **207**

Introduction

This **Legacy Leadership Application Journal** is the practical tool for applying the basic concepts of Legacy Leadership®. Legacy Leadership® is based on The 5 Best Practices, which contain 10 Critical Success Skills each, for a total of 50 competencies. Legacy Leadership® and this application workbook provide a complete structure and framework around which both individuals and whole organizations can become Legacy Leaders, nurturing, promoting and influencing not only today's leaders, but growing tomorrow's as well.

This workbook to apply Legacy Leadership® is an easy and efficient way to spread a successful leadership model throughout an organization, creating an organizational leadership culture. It offers a practical method of learning for leadership development, and skill building for successful leadership in the daily operations of any organization.

*Although this journaling workbook is able to "stand alone" not requiring the use of any additional materials, it is highly recommended that it is paired with the book "**Legacy Leadership: The Leader's Guide to Lasting Greatness**" (2nd Edition) by Sandstrom and Smith, available through most online booksellers. The Legacy Leadership model is fully detailed in that book, so we will just give you a few of the basic highlights and summaries here.*

LEGACY LEADERSHIP® is a comprehensive leadership model for ***individual professionals*** who:

- would like to work within a congruent and consistent leadership system that is well-structured for insuring organizational success.
- would like to have a method for holding themselves and others accountable for success.
- would like to develop personal creativity and become more innovative and flexible.
- would like to be able to see change as a great opportunity and to envision new possibilities with other members of their team.
- would like to become more of a mentor, modeling leadership practices and attitudes to others in their team.
- would like to stretch to become the very best they can be in all areas of life, both professionally and personally.
- would like to inspire others, and be inspired, to see and reach the greatest potentials.
- would like work to be fun, and also promote that environment for others.
- are ready to change their attitudes and break out of old habits to create new successes.
- are willing to make an investment in time and commitment for themselves, and the Company.

LEGACY LEADERSHIP®, and this workbook, serve as a leadership development tool for ***companies and organizations*** that:

- want leadership that sets a clear direction.
- desire an organization-wide leadership standard.
- would like a reputation in the outside corporate world of integrity and employee value.
- want to attract and retain high potential employees.
- would like to be sure the right people are in the right positions for optimum efficiency and output.
- want to increase loyalty among customers.
- want to be known as "the place to work" in the marketplace of talent.
- want higher performance and more measurable outcomes.
- want a healthier bottom line.
- are willing to expand out from old boundaries and learn new patterns for success.
- are willing to make an investment in the future of its employees, its purpose, and its financial goals.

LEGACY LEADERSHIP® outlines and defines the way the organization does business in every meeting, every operation, every project, every level.

This workbook makes it easy to embrace a powerful leadership system throughout an organization by providing the tools for individuals to sustain that culture. Legacy Leadership® was designed for leadership development at all levels both professionally and organizationally. Every employee is a potential leader. Every employee is capable of completing the exercises contained in this workbook, and of becoming true *Legacy Leaders*.

In the first part of this workbook, the basics (the "bare bones" structure) of Legacy Leadership are presented. This is followed by individual development sections for each Best Practice. Again, it is highly recommended this workbook is used in association with the book **"Legacy Leadership: The Leader's Guide to Lasting Greatness."**

What Is Legacy Leadership®?

Legacy Leadership® is the wisdom of the ages structured and packaged for today's - and tomorrow's - leaders. Its truths and Best Practices are timeless, proven keys to sustained significance—and form the foundation for real-time legacy in today's business environment. Legacy Leadership® is a complete program—a philosophy, a process, and a model. Legacy Leadership® is not a leadership style—it is a life system and a way of "being" not just "doing."

This highly adaptable model was developed as the result of over 40 years of the combined experiences of the CoachWorks® principals in individual, corporate, and organizational leadership development. Legacy Leadership® is more than a program. The founders of CoachWorks® International have refined reliable time-honored principles into an intentional, powerful system for success—today and tomorrow. For self and for others.

Are you living your legacy? "Legacy" is commonly thought to be something you leave behind when you're gone. What if you were living your legacy now? What if your vision for the future was evident in everything you do, every day? It can happen.

Drs. Lee Smith and Jeannine Sandstrom developed the Legacy Leadership® program as a result of their work with business leaders in all sectors. When they observed the most common behaviors of successful leaders, they identified the Best Practices that set outstanding leaders apart from their peers. When they listened to the deepest issues that were on leaders' minds, they were matters of legacy. The Legacy Leadership program was developed as a map for ensuring excellence in leadership practices that would enable leaders to leave the legacy they intended.

CoachWorks® International has isolated, defined, and made transferable the practices common to leaders who are able to achieve and sustain success—with people, product, and revenue. Legacy Leadership® is based on 5 Best Practices which are common in all great leaders, whether it be the ancients whose successes leap from the worn pages of history, or the Fortune 500 leaders of today—and will be observed in the leaders of tomorrow.

> *"A business periodical asked a number of corporate chief executives "to look over the horizon of today's headlines," "size up the future," and describe the most pressing tasks that lie beyond the millennium for chief executives. I was invited to do so as well. In my response I wrote, "The three major challenges CEOs will face have little to do with managing the enterprise's tangible assets and everything to do with monitoring the quality of: leadership, the workforce, and relationships."*
>
> Frances Hesselbein,
> "The How To Be Leader."
> <u>The Leader of the Future: New Visions, Strategies, and Practices for the Next Era</u>.
> Jossey-Bass Publishers, San Francisco, CA.

Legacy Leadership® is a philosophy, a model, and a proven process for bringing out individual best, developing other leaders in the organization, establishing organizational leadership culture, and positively impacting the bottom line.

Current leader books and articles cover various aspects and techniques of leadership, but do not deliver a comprehensive model. Legacy Leadership is a complete framework of practices, behaviors, attitudes and values that addresses every aspect of successful leadership.

Legacy Leaders® become students of leadership while focusing on building other leaders who build leaders, who build leaders...

We hear stories every day about the lack of strong leadership talent. Legacy Leadership® is a comprehensive model for developing such talented leaders. It includes competencies and practices with immediate applicability to most every possibility and challenge leaders face today. These practices embrace both vision and accountability for results, as well as methods for creating an environment for team success, strong and dependable relationships, and maximizing the talents of diverse perspectives and strengths.

Many organizations have a set of competencies with which to measure their leader performance; others do not. In either case, Legacy Leadership® provides a sound structure for such competencies to reside. With the structural map of the 5 Best Practices, you have a full and complete picture of the destination your leader development program will go, for you personally, and for those you lead. The basic focus of Legacy Leadership® is on OTHERS, rather than on the leader, in order to develop leaders who then develop other leaders. The outcome is fully developed leaders, both current and emerging, and a greatly enhanced leadership potential within the organization.

Legacy, in this model, is not about building things, but building people. It is about investing in individual leaders who then share what they have learned with others. Legacy is realized in this perpetuating cycle of leadership development by enabling your personal and organizational plan to come alive and thrive. Your best self is offered to others in order to develop their best selves and so on, leaving a multi-generational imprint—a living legacy.

**Leadership Competencies and Critical Success Skills—
The 5 Best Practices of Legacy Leadership®**

Given that leadership can be complex, we have simplified and distinguished five core competency platforms and associated critical success skills for successful leadership. These platforms represent a complete set of observable and measurable behaviors. The behaviors, when used in total, are leverage points for success. We have included those practices of leadership that are essential for every leader, regardless of their industry or level within the organization. There are many leaders in our world, but only those who desire to grow their competencies will be the most successful, influential and effective leaders; and more importantly, leaders whom people desire to follow—*Legacy Leaders®*.

Legacy Leadership® Model

Legacy Leadership is based upon five core competency platforms for successful leadership which we call The 5 Best Practices. Most major leadership models or approaches will find a fit within this balanced framework. We have included those practices of leadership that are essential for every leader, regardless of their industry or level within the organization. These practice areas form the context of the Legacy Leadership® Model™.

1. Holder of Vision and Values™
Direction and Commitment

2. Creator of Collaboration and Innovation™
The environment of working relationships

3. Influencer of Inspiration and Leadership™
Connecting with individuals, the heart of relationships

4. Advocator of Differences and Community™
Distinction and Inclusion

5. Calibrator of Responsibility and Accountability™
Execution and performance

The Essence

	1 Holder of Vision and Values™	2 Creator of Collaboration and Innovation™	3 Influencer of Leadership and Inspiration™	4 Advocator of Differences and Community™	5 Calibrator of Responsibility and Accountability™
DESCRIPTION	Leaders embody/hold company's vision and values, which spell out where company is going and guiding principles by which they will operate. Leaders' behaviors are such that all work is organized around these 2 factors and leadership team, all performance, is measured against them.	Leaders supply environments where team members are comfortable enough to create possibilities greater than they would have alone. The group then discovers new practices, tool or products that changes or improves everything.	Leaders are "trail blazers" with a positive influence so that everyone is lifted up to be the best they can be. Participants are invited (not commanded) to contribute from strengths and are filled with energy to deliver high quality outcomes.	Leaders possess a mindset that all people have unique and compelling contributions to make. Leaders speak up for each person to forward that person's development and progress with the company.	Leaders who demonstrate personal standards of behavior and accountability, who provide clarity about expectations for results and who ensure measurement of progress toward the vision, with an eye for flexibility and mid-course corrections.
CRITICAL FACTORS	MUST BE IN PLACE: • Clear, compelling vision • Values statement • Business objectives • Strategic design • Roadmap and milestones • Communication throughout company of all above • Ways to measure all	MUST BE IN PLACE: • Creative environment • Commitment to innovation • Processes for collaboration • High levels of trust • Process of capturing outcomes	MUST BE IN PLACE: • Positively inspired leaders • Abilities and processes to engage others from strengths • Personal connections • Stories that inspire	MUST BE IN PLACE: • Processes for identifying strengths and styles • Comfort with differing perspectives • Practice inclusion vs exclusion	MUST BE IN PLACE: • Calibration processes vs discipline • Measurements and rewards • Measurements against roadmap and milestones
BARRIERS TO SUCCESS	WHAT PREVENTS SUCCESS? • Lack of commitment • Missing Communication • Lack of Measurements • Focus on short term activity vs long term commitment • Lack of modeling of values by leadership	WHAT PREVENTS SUCCESS? • Mindset for change avoidance • Lack of trust • Lack of inspiration by leader • Lack of methods for discovery • Fear of creative tension	WHAT PREVENTS SUCCESS? • Focus on numbers not people • Not knowing what influences • Fear or mistrust • Previous history with the influencer	WHAT PREVENTS SUCCESS? • Belief systems and biases • Stereotyping • "Rubber stamp" mentality • Avoidance of vulnerability • "Us against them" thinking	WHAT PREVENTS SUCCESS? • Leader not holding self or others accountable • "Either/Or" thinking • Qualifiers that diminish • Exclusion of customer in the measurement mix

Expected Outcomes

	BEST PRACTICE		ORGANIZATIONAL (The Company)	PROFESSIONAL (The Leader)
1	HOLDER	VISION	<ul><li>Clarity of focus</li><li>Strategic implementation against vision</li><li>Consistent communication about focus</li></ul>	<ul><li>Reminds people of what's important</li><li>Clear alignment with followers</li><li>Brings whole self to leadership</li></ul>
		VALUES	<ul><li>Reputation of a company with values</li><li>Congruent guiding principles in the culture</li><li>A culture of integrity</li></ul>	<ul><li>"Walks the Talk" of personal core values</li><li>Has meaning and purpose for efforts</li><li>Models authenticity</li></ul>
2	CREATOR	COLLABORATION	<ul><li>Fosters environment of trust and loyalty</li><li>Breaks down "silos"</li><li>Creates flexibility and adaptability</li></ul>	<ul><li>Puts ego aside to hear brilliance of others</li><li>Builds teams and networks</li><li>Brings out best, asks tough questions</li></ul>
		INNOVATION	<ul><li>Creative energy for competitive advantage</li><li>Fast learning</li><li>Environment of thought leadership</li></ul>	<ul><li>Enhanced personal creativity</li><li>Ability to shift quickly, personal agility</li><li>Embrace change as opportunity</li></ul>
3	INFLUENCER	INSPIRATION	<ul><li>Highly motivating environment</li><li>Encouragement to bring whole self to work</li><li>Employees feel valued for contribution</li></ul>	<ul><li>Is both inspired and inspiring</li><li>Passionate with focused energy</li><li>Models that work is FUN</li></ul>
		LEADERSHIP	<ul><li>Develops emerging leaders at all levels</li><li>Links leadership w/strategic plan</li><li>A systems focus on leadership practices</li></ul>	<ul><li>Stretches to be the best</li><li>Leader competencies developed</li><li>Has a "platform" for actively mentoring</li></ul>
4	ADVOCATOR	DIFFERENCES	<ul><li>Is a "connoisseur" of talent</li><li>Taps abilities of ALL, including "fringes"</li><li>Reduced turnover, greater retention</li></ul>	<ul><li>Discovery of own uniqueness</li><li>Finds own distinguishing strength set</li><li>Learns from those who are different</li></ul>
		COMMUNITY	<ul><li>Reputation attractive to employees</li><li>Greater commitment to community</li><li>Greater sense of authentic purpose</li></ul>	<ul><li>Gets voice heard while hearing others</li><li>Releases old biases, is inclusive</li><li>Makes alliances between leader and led</li></ul>
5	CALIBRATOR	RESPONSIBILITY	<ul><li>Right people in right jobs</li><li>Optimized strengths</li><li>Consistent standards</li></ul>	<ul><li>Is the right leader for the job</li><li>Produces excellent results, value added</li><li>Requires everyone's personal responsibility</li></ul>
		ACCOUNTABILITY	<ul><li>High level of achievement</li><li>Measurable outcomes</li><li>Loyal customers</li></ul>	<ul><li>Holds self and others accountable</li><li>Communicates expectations</li><li>Calibrates regularly and consistently</li></ul>

Definitions

DEFINITIONS			EXPLANATION

Holder of Vision and Values™ — 1

HOLDER	VISION	VALUES	
One who "keeps" in hand those things that are important, by embracing and encouraging their remembrance.	A clear view and understanding of realizable goals, plans and intentions.	Those things considered right, worthwhile and desirable—the basis of guiding principles and standards.	This Best Practice is about direction and commitment. The term "holder" indicates that the leader lives the vision and values while measuring every action against both. The leader then provides consistent focus and direction. The critical success skills include: integration of vision/values into all responsibilities, having a well-defined strategic plan, team translation of vision and values, establishing milestones and benchmarks, modeling the practice, developing the potential of others to pull out the best in them, and effectively communicating and sustaining organizational vision/values.

Creator of Collaboration and Innovation™ — 2

CREATOR	COLLABORATION	INNOVATION	
One who causes something to "come into being" through original or inventive means.	The process of working together to achieve common goals instead of personal agenda.	The introduction of something new and different to the process of achieving goals	This Best Practice is about creating a positive environment for working relationships. The term "creator" indicates the leader's ability to create a learning trusting environment where collaboration and innovation can occur. The critical success skills include abilities to: unleash innovation, listen masterfully, learn from others, be aware of the bigger picture, discern when change needs to occur, and being a masterful facilitator.

Influencer of Inspiration and Leadership™ — 3

INFLUENCER	INSPIRATION	LEADERSHIP	
One who brings about a desired effect in others, by direct or indirect means.	The process of animating, motivating or encouraging others to reach new levels of achievement.	The process of guiding and directing others to shared success.	This Best Practice is about making connections with individuals—the heart of relationships as well as leadership. The term "influencer" indicates the leader's ability to influence and inspire for positive relationships. The critical success skills include abilities to: influence positively, demonstrate high levels of emotional intelligence, bring out the best in people by developing them fully, focus on others rather than self, make tough decisions with minimal people impact, and be humble while holding resolve to accomplish stated goals.

Advocator of Differences and Community™ — 4

ADVOCATOR	DIFFERENCES	COMMUNITY	
One who stands in support of a cause, a practice or a person on its or their behalf.	Those qualities that distinguish people or things from other people or things.	A group of people with shared interest working together to achieve shared success.	This Best Practice is about distinguishing individual strengths and inclusion of differing perspectives. The term "advocator" indicates the leader's ability to support and stand for strengths-based talent. The critical success skills include abilities to: be an advocator of individuals, be a connoisseur of talent, insist on teams with diverse perspectives and abilities, stand for cross-functional development and collaboration, recognize community impact, and promote an inclusive environment united toward a common focus.

Calibrator of Responsibility and Accountability™ — 5

CALIBRATOR	RESPONSIBILITY	ACCOUNTABILITY	
One who "sets the mark" for the quantitative measurement of success/acceptance.	The ability to respond correctly to—and meet—stated expectations.	The obligation to justify conduct, conditions or circumstances.	This Best Practice is about execution and performance measured against vision and values. The term "calibrator" indicates constant vigilance, with possible adjustments, of progress toward accomplishing responsibilities and accountabilities. The critical success skills include abilities to: execute successfully, maintain a "finger on the pulse" for status measurement, require peak performance, provide feedback and coaching, have clearly defined action plans, model a sense of urgency in getting things done and respond to change, be alert to trends, and gain commitment to follow-through.

The Being and Doing of Legacy Leadership and Aerial Views

Being and Doing

Each of the 5 Best Practices has three components: one part BEING, and two parts DOING. Most leadership models have a list of competencies, skills and actions that contribute to good leadership. But great leaders don't just DO, they ARE. As we initially sought to label the 5 Best Practices, it became difficult to apply a simple label to include all the inherent components. We finally settled on labels that actually said what was meant, and were not merely coined terms or jargon. Too often people focus merely on the doing of leadership. It is vital to consider BOTH aspects of being and doing. BEING involves a certain consciousness, awareness of who the leader is.

Best Practice 1: **HOLDER OF VISION AND VALUES**™   **(BEING: Holder)**
Great leaders are conscious guardians of both personal and organizational vision and values. It becomes part of who they are, and guides all they do. BEING a Holder implies understanding the necessity of never allowing vision and values to slip out of focus or priority. Merely having vision, or having values is not enough. They must be intentionally held. A Legacy Leader® is very clear about his or her own personal core vision and values, which are the driving forces for their leadership. Leadership is not just about doing vision, and doing values—professionally or organizationally. A Legacy Leader® LIVES them, preserves them, and relies upon them as a guide.

Best Practice 2: **CREATOR of COLLABORATION and INNOVATION**™   **(BEING: Creator)**
Collaboration and Innovation don't happen by themselves. They must be encouraged, nurtured, with opportunities created by leaders. This is not about being *creative*, it is about being a *creator*, one who instinctively creates opportunities where collaboration and innovation can flourish. A creator actually causes something to come into being, in this case collaboration and innovation, sometimes through inventive means. The Legacy Leader® becomes an active "opportunity seeker" and possibility thinker. This is an attitude of leadership, not just a leadership action.

Best Practice 3: **INFLUENCER of INSPIRATION AND LEADERSHIP**™   **(BEING: Influencer)**
A Legacy Leader® understands that we cannot NOT influence, and therefore becomes an intentional influencer. It is about having a consciousness that all that we do influences, even when we aren't aware of it. In all we do, we will either influence in a positive or negative way. The Legacy Leader® makes a choice to BE an influencer in a positive way, regardless of the situation or circumstances. This becomes a way of life, a way of being. This awareness tempers our behavior both personally and professionally.

Best Practice 4: **ADVOCATOR of DIFFERENCES and COMMUNITY**™   **(BEING: Advocator)**
An advocator is one who stands firm in support. It is about BEING someone who is courageous enough to take a stand, and stay standing. It means having a well-defined sense of right, and the internal strength to defend it. A leader cannot DO this, if he or she cannot BE it. It is an unfortunate truth in business today that we do not find too many people who are so clear about who they are that they are willing to take a firm stand regardless of consequences. But a Legacy Leader® is a ready advocate for what is right, which often involves risk. The word advocator was selected because it carries more strength than defender or supporter. This is about internal commitment to causes, practices and people.

Best Practice 5: **CALIBRATOR of RESPONSIBILITY and ACCOUNTABILITY**™   **(BEING: Calibrator)**
A calibrator is one who is clear about standards, vision, values, and what is right both personally and organizationally, and measures all behavior against them. This is an ongoing internal process that never stops. It is a natural, conscious and continual setting of the "mark" and adjusting what is necessary to hit it consistently. It implies a sense of awareness, measurement and appropriate adjustment. Again, it is not just doing, it is being vigilant, accountable, responsible, thoughtful and nimble, with a constant eye on the target. A Legacy Leader® is a human thermostat, always measuring the environment and adjusting as necessary.

Aerial Views

The following pages present a condensed view of the basics of each of the 5 Best Practices of Legacy Leadership®. These "Aerial Views" are presented in two-column layout, with one part of the DOING in one column, and the other part of the DOING in the other column. Definitions for the BEING components of the 5 Best Practices can be found in previous tables, and above.

Holder of Vision and Values™

A HOLDER "keeps in hand" those things that are important, embracing and encouraging their remembrance.

BP1 - Aerial View

Definition	**VISION** is a clear view and understanding of realizable goals, plans and intentions.	**VALUES** are those things considered right, worthwhile, and desirable—the basis of guiding principles and standards.
What it IS: The Legacy Leader will:	<ul><li>hold vision by being clear on both personal and organizational vision and by measuring all ideas, decisions, commitment and actions against the organization's vision template.</li><li>encourage, promote and protect such organizational vision by embracing and encouraging its remembrance.</li><li>establish and maintain this vision "holding" so that it becomes foundational to all activities.</li></ul>	<ul><li>hold values by being clear on both personal and organizational guiding principles and standards and by measuring all ideas, decisions, commitment and actions against the organization's values template.</li><li>encourage, promote and protect these values by embracing them, modeling them and encouraging their remembrance.</li><li>establish and maintain this values "holding" so that it becomes foundational to all activities.</li></ul>
What it is NOT:	<ul><li>Vague reference to non-measurable goals</li><li>A ruler to "slap hands"</li><li>Harboring "secret information"</li></ul>	<ul><li>Enforcing "rules"</li><li>Merely acknowledging a behavior code</li><li>Self righteousness</li></ul>
Factors for Success (what must be in place)	<ul><li>Clear compelling organizational vision in writing</li><li>Excellent communication of vision throughout organization</li><li>Ways to measure vision</li><li>Roadmap and milestones</li><li>Compelling strategic design throughout organization</li><li>Knowledge of personal vision/match to organizational vision</li></ul>	<ul><li>Fully developed values statement and guiding principles that are clearly defined</li><li>Organization-wide communication of values</li><li>Measurement methods</li><li>Employee clarity and acceptance of values</li><li>Attitude of values underlying all work</li></ul>
Challenges (Potential Barriers)	<ul><li>No existing written or communicated organizational vision</li><li>Teammates are not invested or interested in organizational vision – are self interested</li><li>Existing vision is not compelling, inspiring</li><li>Existing vision is not measurable</li></ul>	<ul><li>No established organizational values, guiding principles</li><li>Leadership does not model values</li><li>Individual "renegades" as exception to expected behavior</li><li>Existing values not "owned" by employees</li><li>Individuals with conflicting personal values</li></ul>
Behaviors and Competencies **The Holder of this will...**	<ul><li>have a well-defined personal vision.</li><li>clearly understand organization's vision and use it as a foundational purpose for all efforts.</li><li>have clear alignment with organization's vision, and its relationship with all individuals, teams, and activities.</li><li>bring his or her whole self to this leadership model.</li><li>consistently communicate and strategize around, and measure performance against organizational vision.</li><li>encourage others to create their own vision.</li><li>protect the vision from being diminished.</li><li>provide consistent focus and direction.</li><li>make vision exciting, help it come alive in daily activities.</li></ul>	<ul><li>have a set of clearly defined personal values.</li><li>"walk the talk" of personal core values.</li><li>encourage others to develop, define and live personal values.</li><li>understand the organization's values and use them as a foundational purpose for all efforts.</li><li>understand and encourage consistent use of organizational guiding principles that are observable, measurable, and replicable by others.</li><li>protect personal/organizational values from eroding.</li><li>model authenticity. Personal, professional life seamless.</li><li>encourage values-driven achievement in others.</li></ul>
LegacyShifts™	<ul><li>FROM fuzzy TO focused</li><li>FROM "wandering lost" TO following roadmaps, milestones</li><li>FROM no personal direction TO well-defined personal vision and goals</li></ul>	<ul><li>FROM lack of operational policies TO well communicated guiding principles</li><li>FROM bad or no reputation TO reputation for excellence</li><li>FROM "cover-ups" TO open pride</li></ul>
Legacy Steps	1. Determine organization's vision statement(s). Re-state, re-work, re-affirm as necessary for clear communication. 2. Plan how you will explain, communicate this easily. 3. Openly, frequently communicate vision at every level, encouraging buy-in and cooperation. 4. Hold up every decision/action to organizational vision. Discard those that do not match up. 5. Be sure vision is kept as foundation of every project and goal until it becomes an automatic "reflex." 6. Be able to easily articulate the organizational (as well as personal) vision for both. 7. Formulate personal vision in written and measurable format, internalize for use in achievement of organizational vision. 8. Bring whole self to your leadership. 9. Understand that what you do and say today shapes the future. 10. Make organizational vision compelling, inspiring to others.	1. Determine organization's values statement(s). How does this company want to be known in the workplace? 2. Openly, frequently communicate values at every level, encouraging buy-in, cooperation. 3. Hold up every decision or action to organizational values. Discard non-matches. No compromise. 4. Be sure organizational values are reflected in every activity so that it becomes automatic "reflex." 5. Be able to easily articulate organizational/personal values—talk is important, but walk is loudest. 6. Alert team members when values may be compromised. 7. Avoid self righteousness! 8. Remember, organization's reputation is your reputation. 9. Determine how you will uphold personal core values when and if they do not match organization's values. 10. Don't "cover up" mistakes, or compromise values.

Creator of Collaboration and Innovation™

A CREATOR causes something to "come into being" often through original or inventive means.

BP2 - Aerial View

	COLLABORATION is the process of working together to achieve common goals instead of personal agenda.	**INNOVATION** is the introduction of something new and different to the process of achieving goals.
Definition		
What it IS: The Legacy Leader will:	<ul><li>create collaboration by gathering people with differing perspectives, talents, gifts, and attitudes for the purpose of creating something bigger, better and more significant than any one of them could have done alone.</li><li>encourage, promote and protect such collaboration through a variety of inventive means.</li><li>establish and maintain this collaborative process so that it becomes foundational to all activities.</li></ul>	<ul><li>create innovation by challenging current thinking and assumptions, encouraging the creation and installation of better ways and ideas, and by role-modeling for the team or community imaginative and inventive visualization beyond the present reality. Innovation is the product of creative collaboration.</li><li>encourage, promote and protect such collaborative innovation through a variety of inventive means.</li><li>maintain this innovative process so that it becomes foundational to all activities.</li></ul>
What it is NOT:	<ul><li>Forced cooperation</li><li>Impromptu Brainstorming</li><li>Fostered Competition</li></ul>	<ul><li>Visioning and Futuristic Thinking</li><li>Creativity</li><li>Change for Change Sake</li></ul>
Factors for Success (what must be in place)	<ul><li>High levels of trust</li><li>A "team" mindset</li><li>Processes for building collaboration, capturing outcomes, follow through</li><li>Personal responsibility</li></ul>	<ul><li>A creative environment</li><li>A commitment to innovation</li><li>High levels of trust</li><li>Framework for collaboration</li><li>"No boundaries" in thought processes</li></ul>
Challenges (Potential Barriers)	<ul><li>No process for collaboration (environment that does not allow for free exchange of ideas)</li><li>Teammates self-interested, not community interested</li><li>Employee disrespect</li><li>Lack of trust</li><li>Lack of collaborative skills or mindset</li><li>Resistance to creating something new *(stuck in comfort zone)*</li></ul>	<ul><li>Fear of change</li><li>Focus on past or present</li><li>Fear of real success</li><li>Dissenters/Narrow thinkers *("We can't do that." "That won't work.")*</li></ul>
Behaviors and Competencies **The Creator of this will...**	<ul><li>look for ways to create a collaborative circle among existing teams, structures, etc.</li><li>be inventive, encouraging communication and openness.</li><li>put aside ego to hear the brilliance of others.</li><li>be specific about shared goals and interests.</li><li>bring out the best in others.</li><li>ask the tough questions and hear the answers.</li><li>create an atmosphere of flexibility and adaptability</li><li>put aside fears of creative tension.</li></ul>	<ul><li>do a variety of things to enhance their own personal creativity.</li><li>look for areas where mistrust may be a hurdle, and work to remove it.</li><li>open closed "boxes" for others to see inside and outside.</li><li>generate excitement for shared innovation and results.</li><li>challenge thinking "outside the norm."</li><li>have the ability to shift quickly – personal "agility."</li><li>embrace change as great opportunity.</li><li>encourage continual learning.</li></ul>
LegacyShifts™	<ul><li>FROM judgment TO curiosity</li><li>FROM "ho hum" meetings TO "ah hah!" sessions</li><li>FROM suspicion TO trust</li></ul>	<ul><li>FROM ordinary TO extraordinary</li><li>FROM focus on past TO focus on future</li><li>FROM fear of change TO embracing the new</li></ul>
Legacy Steps	1. Be respectful. 2. Listen thoroughly. 3. Honor differences of opinion. 4. Create atmosphere where everyone is heard, feels free to contribute. 5. Encourage everyone's participation. 6. Communicate expectations of collaboration. 7. Give equal ranking to all ideas. Set judgment aside. Be open minded. 8. Focus on "greater good" of organization. 9. Become familiar with strengths of teammates, perspectives, gifts, points of view, etc. 10. Make interaction fun, invigorating. 11. Speak the truth with respect and clarity.	1. Clearly identify challenge(s). 2. Gather together a group of cross-functional individuals with unique perspectives and responsibilities. 3. Clearly establish the process. 4. Set the ground rules, parameters, boundaries, etc. 5. Openly work collaboratively to design process. 6. Do not judge ideas until all innovative thinking is on the table. 7. All ideas in writing and all process documented, logged for review. 8. Share everything.

Influencer of Inspiration and Leadership™

An INFLUENCER brings about a desired effect in others, either by direct or indirect means.

BP3 - Aerial View

	INSPIRATION is the process of animating, motivating or encouraging others to reach new levels of achievement.	LEADERSHIP is the process of guiding and directing others to shared success.
Definition		
What it IS: The Legacy Leader will:	■ Influence inspiration by creating an environment that brings people to life and fills others with energy. In doing so, others will then bring inspiration and life to the organization. ■ encourage, promote and protect such inspiration by encouraging ongoing and lasting positive energy and passion in others by providing a consistent model. ■ establish and maintain this inspirational process so that it becomes foundational to all activities.	■ Influence the leadership both OF and IN others by leading through positive rather than negative influence, AND by encouraging the discovery and development of positive leadership styles in others. We believe everyone is a leader, and as such, should have positive influential leaders as role models, and be encouraged in their own leadership style development. ■ encourage, promote and protect this influential leadership by always providing a positive role model, and by creating opportunities for learning and discovery of personal leadership styles. ■ maintain this influential leadership process so that it becomes foundational to all activities.
What it is NOT:	■ Simply motivation ■ "Pumping Up" ■ Putting on a "happy face"	■ "Cloning" leaders ■ Political correctness ■ Kingdom or Empire Building
Factors for Success (what must be in place)	■ Strong sense of vision and values ■ Desire to encourage and inspire others ■ Understanding of others' strengths ■ Mental "library" of stories that inspire ■ Understanding of what inspires self, and others ■ Desire and ability to live a role model for others ■ Understanding of own personal passion	■ Ability/desire to influence others in a positive way ■ Ability to look at challenges as opportunities for growth ■ A solid working knowledge of the cutting edge technology of various leadership models and styles ■ Ability and desire to build relationships ■ Consistent positive thinking ■ Desire to mentor ■ More importance on development of others, rather than self ■ Clear vision and values (personal and organizational)
Challenges (Potential Barriers)	■ Soul-less environment (heart is not included in processes) ■ Teammates are self-interested, not others-interested ■ Employee disrespect for fellow workers ■ Lack of trust ■ Self-protective barriers ■ Organizational rules—separation of business and personal ■ Organizational emphasis on numbers	■ Hidden organizational or personal agendas ■ Lack of knowledge of leadership styles, skills, models ■ Insufficient trust between leader and potential leader ■ Lack of respect for others ■ Organizational command-and-control rather than nurturing structure
Behaviors and Competencies **The Influencer of this will...**	■ know him or her self well, and what inspires them. ■ be self-inspired, and know what inspires others. ■ work to discover strengths of others to better inspire them. ■ express a positive, powerful hope for the future - both personally and organizationally. ■ build trust in others. ■ develop a personal repertoire of inspirational stories. ■ keep the heart included in all processes. ■ connect personally/others, value individually and corporately. ■ walk a daily path, with even attitude, consistent energy and influential encouragement. ■ have passion and consistency.	■ have a positive attitude at all (okay, most!) times. ■ use positive and uplifting language, even in crisis or other challenging moments. ■ be able to make the right choices in difficult situations. ■ have excellent internal character, principles and values. ■ have an excellent working knowledge of cutting edge leadership technologies, model, styles and language. ■ provide appropriate opportunities to develop the leadership abilities, skills and styles in those they lead. ■ invite rather than commands. ■ seek moments each day to uplift, enhance growth of others. ■ instill confidence rather than destroying it.
LegacyShifts™	■ FROM heartless TO heartfelt ■ FROM pulling teeth TO sustained energy and passion ■ FROM bringing down TO lifting up	■ FROM personal power TO empowering others ■ FROM a negative attitude TO a BE-attitude ■ FROM isolationism TO relationalism
Legacy Steps	1. Develop ability to successfully influence others to self-motivation, self-inspiration. 2. Discover strengths of others. 3. Learn what inspires others. 4. Develop an attitude of inspiration. 5. Connect personally with others on all levels. 6. Develop and tell stories (at appropriate times) that inspire. 7. Challenge and encourage others to work from their strengths. 8. Focus on living a model of consistent inspiration for others. 9. Discard old ideas of motivation. 10. Continue personal learning, and being inspired by others. 11. Learn how to consistently bring out the best in others.	1. CHOOSE to be positive. 2. Open doors, take down walls, and break through any barriers between yourself and others. 3. Build knowledge of various leadership models and styles. Determine what works and what doesn't. Model what works. 4. Work at building the trust of fellow workers. 5. Get to really know your team members. 6. Diffuse conflict and confrontation with positive energy. 7. Honestly evaluate own leadership intentions/style. Throw out self-centered, develop other-centered aspects. 8. Respect others—always, and regardless! 9. Consider everyone you work with a potential leader. 10. Take care of yourself physically and spiritually!

Advocator of Differences and Community™

An ADVOCATOR stands in support of a cause, a practice or a person on its or their behalf.

	DIFFERENCES are those qualities that distinguish people or things from other people or things.	COMMUNITY is a group of people with shared interest working together to achieve shared success.
Definition		
What it IS: The Legacy Leader will:	<ul><li>advocate differences by seeking relationships with team members, by discovering, acknowledging, and accepting differences in those relationships, and by promoting individual strengths and perspectives for the greater whole of the organization.</li><li>encourage, promote and protect such advocacy by drawing together individuals who contribute diverse perspectives for a greater good, and will model the endorsement and leveraging of differences into added value for the whole.</li><li>establish and maintain this advocacy so that it becomes foundational to all activities.</li></ul>	<ul><li>advocate promoting and combining of differences into a unified whole, and then stand in support of this community as it builds relationships— from within and without the organization— that enlarge and expand the growth of the community, and the success of the organization.</li><li>encourage, promote, protect and advocate for this community by helping individuals and teams discover strengths in both commonality and differences that can be instrumental in the growth of the individual, the community and the organization, and by modeling an attitude of connectedness and inclusion.</li><li>maintain advocacy of community so it becomes foundational to all activities.</li></ul>
What it is NOT:	<ul><li>Equal Employment Opportunity</li><li>The token "oddball"</li><li>Giving "lip service"</li></ul>	<ul><li>Manipulation</li><li>"Rally 'round the flag" time</li><li>Forced inclusion</li></ul>
Factors for Success (what must be in place)	<ul><li>Acknowledgement of the importance and benefit of differences</li><li>Environment that promotes relationships</li><li>Openness to diverse perspectives</li><li>Complete lack of prejudices or other difference-limiting mindsets</li><li>Passion for learning, discovery</li><li>Individual egos that take a backseat to wholeness</li><li>Lack of labels and stereotypes</li></ul>	<ul><li>Good team-building environment</li><li>Acknowledgement that all parts needed to make the whole</li><li>Management that promotes community</li><li>Understanding of the strength afforded in differences</li><li>Keen desire to know others as people, not pawns</li><li>Understanding that as one grows and succeeds, ALL do.</li><li>Ability to unite differences into community process</li><li>Desire to embrace and incorporate diversity in all activities</li><li>Excellent, consistent, and clear communication</li></ul>
Challenges (Potential Barriers)	<ul><li>Labels and prejudices</li><li>Turf protection ("them" against "us")</li><li>Comfort zones</li><li>"Rubber stamp" or "cookie cutter" mentality</li><li>Non-inclusive belief systems</li><li>"First sight" snap judgments</li><li>Inability to see beyond appearances</li></ul>	<ul><li>Hidden, or even stated, organizational or personal agendas</li><li>Organizational or personal lack of concern for others</li><li>A need to get the "credit" for successes</li><li>Lack of respect for others</li><li>Command-and-control rather than relational environment</li><li>Inability to see the "trees" for the forest</li><li>Personal, departmental or organizational "walls"</li><li>Communication deficiencies</li></ul>
Behaviors and Competencies The Advocator of this will...	<ul><li>promote differences and value them for the whole.</li><li>know own biases, stereotypes and labels, seek to overcome.</li><li>know how he or she is different.</li><li>discover how others see the world and individual situations.</li><li>be curious about differences, desire to learn more about them.</li><li>reframe how they think and how they approach people who are "different" from themselves.</li><li>practice active and interested listening.</li><li>recap, summarize conversation for clarity</li><li>seek common ground/good in environment of differences.</li><li>take time, have courage to go beyond comfort zone w/others.</li><li>practice being comfortable around those who previously evoked "discomfort."</li></ul>	<ul><li>always look for the strengths of individuals to add to the success of the whole.</li><li>see beyond boundaries of individuals, teams or departments.</li><li>always have the success of the whole in mind.</li><li>know about perspectives/strengths from all sources.</li><li>actively seek to lift up others, even those "outside" immediate corporate or departmental lines.</li><li>be aware of added benefits of inclusion.</li><li>help others discover/value own strengths, potential contributions.</li><li>have identified own strengths.</li><li>communicate well and often with all parts of the whole.</li><li>defend, support and speak up for their community.</li></ul>
LegacyShifts™	<ul><li>FROM "us against them" TO Esprit de corps</li><li>FROM "he doesn't have a clue" TO "what can he share?"</li><li>FROM individuals TO relationships</li></ul>	<ul><li>FROM exclusion TO inclusion</li><li>FROM the "darkness beyond" TO enlightened communication</li><li>FROM scattered pieces TO a healthy whole</li></ul>
Legacy Steps	<ol><li>Set aside your ego.</li><li>Discover/overcome personal biases/prejudices/stereotypes.</li><li>Actively seek out differences and the strengths within them.</li><li>Look for common ground.</li><li>Reframe how you think/approach "different."</li><li>Take time and effort to understand others.</li><li>Become an active and eager listener.</li><li>Actively seek opinions of those who may think differently, and value them.</li><li>Design conversations/meetings to be inclusive, then recap.</li><li>Remember that you don't have all the answers.</li><li>Discard old ideas of territorialism and self-protection.</li></ol>	<ol><li>CHOOSE to be inclusive.</li><li>Open doors, take down walls, break through any barriers.</li><li>Acknowledge and respect the contribution of others.</li><li>Help all discover strengths/potential contribution to whole.</li><li>Evaluate existing communication protocol/habits, work to widen circle, increase frequency and informative content.</li><li>Share information outside perceived department/team.</li><li>Discover your own unique strengths and perspectives.</li><li>Remember you are serving the vision of whole organization.</li><li>Support/defend the community as a whole, expose activities or behaviors that do not do this.</li><li>Be a leader who enables rather than hobbles growth.</li></ol>

Calibrator of Responsibility and Accountability™

A CALIBRATOR "sets the mark," determining the quantitative measurement of acceptance.

 BP5 - Aerial View

	RESPONSIBILITY is the ability to respond correctly to—and meet—stated expectations.	ACCOUNTABILITY is the obligation to explain or justify conduct, conditions or circumstances.
Definition		
What it IS: The Legacy Leader will:	<ul><li>calibrate responsibility by demonstrating (and stating) standards of behavior, providing clarity about expectations of results, and by ensuring measurement of progress towards vision.</li><li>encourage, promote and protect such calibration of responsibility by adjustments for new information and change, providing a consistent role model, and by celebration of accomplished results.</li><li>establish and maintain this calibration so that it becomes foundational to all activities.</li></ul>	<ul><li>calibrate accountability by defining those things for which all are responsible, including themselves, and by providing a measurement system and process to evaluate the success of accomplishments and results.</li><li>encourage, promote, protect and calibrate such accountability by providing a role model for personal responsibility, standards for behavior and results and the consistent milestone marking and evaluation of the process toward expected outcome.</li><li>maintain this calibration of accountability so that it becomes foundational to all activities.</li></ul>
What it is NOT:	<ul><li>Discipline</li><li>Being the "Hall Monitor"</li><li>A Rule Book</li></ul>	<ul><li>Being "called on the carpet"</li><li>Pointing fingers or playing the "blame game"</li><li>The "end justifies the means"</li></ul>
Factors for Success (what must be in place)	<ul><li>Leaders who provide consistent role models of acceptable behavior</li><li>Clear expectations</li><li>Stated and understood vision and values</li><li>Desire to develop others</li><li>The right people in the right jobs</li><li>Excellent communication system</li><li>Measurement systems</li></ul>	<ul><li>Clarity</li><li>Modeling of personal responsibility</li><li>Respect for others, desire to develop others</li><li>Clear standards of behavior, expectations and accountabilities</li><li>Inclusiveness</li><li>Process of measurement</li><li>Identified levels of accountability (individual, team, dept., etc.)</li><li>Excellent, consistent, and clear communication</li></ul>
Challenges (Potential Barriers)	<ul><li>Leaders that do not fulfill their own responsibilities</li><li>Unstated or unclear expectations, vision and values</li><li>No process for evaluation and guidance</li><li>Lack of compassion and caring for people</li><li>Poor placement and matching of people with responsibilities</li><li>No understanding of calibration vs. discipline</li><li>No measurement systems</li></ul>	<ul><li>Leaders not holding self accountable</li><li>No standards, no measurement process, no roadmap</li><li>Qualifiers and exceptions to accountability</li><li>Lack of respect for others</li><li>Either/or thinking</li><li>Forgetting the customer</li><li>Communication deficiencies</li></ul>
Behaviors and Competencies **The Calibrator of this will...**	<ul><li>have clearly defined vision/values, for self and organization.</li><li>know instinctively what is acceptable/"right" behavior, or not.</li><li>help insure that the right people are in the right positions.</li><li>know how to celebrate accomplishment of goals and vision.</li><li>make constant comparisons to and checks against vision and values and other stated milestones.</li><li>focus on what went right and what can be done differently, instead of what went wrong.</li><li>hold themselves responsible first.</li><li>plan for adjustments in standards as a result of new information/changes, but never compromise vision/values.</li><li>provide a consistent role model of expected behavior.</li><li>ensure measurement of progress toward the vision.</li><li>make no exceptions to expectations for responsible behavior.</li></ul>	<ul><li>respect others.</li><li>realize that accountabilities are shared.</li><li>provide a consistent role model of personal accountability.</li><li>set, communicate expectations, milestones, measurement.</li><li>regularly measure accountabilities and compare against existing vision and values.</li><li>understand this is a growth process, not a place for blaming.</li><li>Provide tools (content, context, resources) so a worker can learn and have all that is needed to fulfill responsibilities.</li><li>focus on employees, ask employees to focus on themselves and customer, vendor, or other organizational vision.</li><li>ensure people do those things for which they are responsible, and share responsibility when outcomes fall short of vision.</li><li>be a directional leader.</li></ul>
LegacyShifts™	<ul><li>FROM "what went wrong" TO "how can we do it better"</li><li>FROM do your own thing TO the responsible thing</li><li>FROM mismatched TO perfect match</li></ul>	<ul><li>FROM worker TO owner</li><li>FROM "it's on your head" TO "it's on our shoulders"</li><li>FROM doing my job TO celebrating our achievement</li></ul>
Legacy Steps	<ol><li>Be responsible, expect the same of everyone else.</li><li>Observe/optimize employee performance by ensuring the right people are in the right positions.</li><li>Acknowledge all contributions and celebrate all successes.</li><li>Keep ongoing comparison of all behaviors to vision/values.</li><li>Inspire acceptable behavior by providing right role model.</li><li>Establish roadmaps and targeted milestones for measurement of progress toward vision.</li><li>Dwell on the present and the future, not the past.</li><li>Make all perceived "failures" into opportunities/challenges.</li><li>Make appropriate adjustments to new information/changes.</li><li>Be sure all expectations are clearly communicated.</li><li>Make no exceptions</li></ol>	<ol><li>Hold yourself accountable at all times.</li><li>Set and communicate clear standards.</li><li>Communicate community accountability—no exceptions.</li><li>Remind: highest goal of accountability to satisfy the customer, vendor, or other target of organizational vision.</li><li>Encourage frequent personal accountability checks.</li><li>Perform regular community process accountability.</li><li>Insure frequent/clear communication w/ all parts of whole.</li><li>Encourage relationship building, but not "cliques."</li><li>Understand differences between short-term and long-term performance outcomes.</li><li>Work to keep community in partnership and ownership of overall process, willing to be accountable together.</li></ol>

The Critical Success Skills (CSS)

To enhance the practical application of Legacy Leadership®, each of the 5 Best Practices lists 10 Critical Success Skills. These skills contain the competencies, attitudes and behaviors which are the hallmark of great leaders. Each of these 50 Critical Success Skills (CSS) is detailed in a Drill Down page in this workbook.

Best Practice 1: Holder of Vision and Values™
1. Consistently reinforce the organization's vision and values.
2. Intentionally model guiding principles in everything, with everyone.
3. Personally integrate organization's vision in all responsibilities.
4. Have well-defined strategic plan for accomplishing vision.
5. Enable team to translate organizational vision, and align daily responsibilities with organizational goals.
6. Establish measurable milestones congruent with vision.
7. Ensure that organizational values are integrated into how organization does business.
8. Clearly identify personal values; "walk the talk" in everything.
9. Place importance on developing others.
10. Effectively communicate, sustain processes to achieve vision and values.

Best Practice 2: Creator of Collaboration and Innovation™
1. Create innovative and sound possibilities for the organization.
2. Foster learning, trusting environment for true collaboration and innovation.
3. Masterfully listen for both what is said, what is not said.
4. Be comfortable not knowing "the answers" and learn from individual perspectives.
5. Draw out differing perspectives and believe disagreement is a learning opportunity.
6. Ask timely, tough questions while keeping in mind the big picture.
7. Set the tone for thinking beyond the present for innovative future.
8. Project how ideas will play out in the organization and marketplace.
9. Discern, and assist others to understand, when change needs to happen and when it does not.
10. Masterfully facilitate conversations where everyone contributes best thinking toward task/goal.

Best Practice 3: Influencer of Inspiration and Leadership™
1. Be adept at developing, maintaining relationships.
2. Use emotional intelligence, positive energy to influence others.
3. Choose to model positive perspective in all situations.
4. Bring out the best in people.
5. Constantly acknowledge and recognize attributes and contributions of others.
6. Intentionally delegate for development of others.
7. Lead with constant focus on showcasing others, not self.
8. Have ability and courage to take risks and inspire others to follow.
9. Be able to make tough decisions with minimal negative impact
10. Lead with humility and fierce resolve to accomplish goals through others.

Best Practice 4: Advocator of Differences and Community™
1. Able to take a stand for a person, practice or cause.
2. Constantly raise visibility of individuals by mentoring/developing them.
3. Advocate for a strengths-based culture.
4. Be a connoisseur of talent, recognizing, valuing and utilizing the best each person has to offer.
5. Insist on building teams with diverse approaches and capabilities.
6. Look for/create cross-functional opportunities to develop unique talent.
7. Promote inter-departmental collaboration, rather than "silo" orientation.
8. Consider impact of actions on greater community (beyond organization).
9. Maintain ongoing dialogue/involvement with internal/external communities.
10. Promote inclusive environment to unite toward common focus.

Best Practice 5: Calibrator of Responsibility and Accountability™
1. Execute strategic plan; use appropriate checks and balances to reach goals.
2. Have "finger on pulse" of organization, know milestone status.
3. Have team members clear about position responsibilities and how they fit into direction and deliverables.
4. Require peak performance and support all with appropriate resources.
5. Provide regular feedback/coaching, take action when low performance.
6. Have clearly defined personal and organizational accountabilities.
7. Have clearly developed action plan with benchmarks, milestones and provisions for adjustments.
8. Model sense of urgency for accomplishment and response to change.
9. Be alert to trends which may affect results; recalibrate where necessary.
10. Gain commitment from team with established accountabilities, appropriate consequences/rewards.

The Legacy Leadership® Logo

In this workbook, the Legacy Leadership® logo is seen in black and white only, in 5 square blocks in this formation:

It is obviously representative of the 5 Best Practices. However, the original logo was designed in color *(as seen on the back cover of this book)* and the colors may be helpful in recalling the 5 Best Practices.

We are often asked about the colors used in the Legacy Leadership® logo and model. Do they have significance? We wanted bright, bold, crisp and clean colors for this leadership model—well defined, highly visible and not muted—just like our leadership and our legacy should be. That was the primary motivator for selecting these colors. The colors were also identified with each of the 5 Best Practices in order to provide some easily remembered association.

Yellow, bright and "sunny," is often associated with light and vision. **Yellow is the color of Best Practice 1: Holder of Vision and Values**™. The Legacy Leader® holds and sustains the vision, aligning it with values (personally, professionally, and organizationally). Without this "light," goals remain in the dark. The Legacy Leader® carries the light of vision everywhere. This Best Practice is about direction and commitment.

Blue is the color of cloudless skies. It reminds us of great expanses, unlimited horizons and rich opportunities. For this reason, **blue has been assigned to Best Practice 2: Creator of Collaboration and Innovation**™. A creator brings something into being through original and inventive means. A Legacy Leader® creates collaboration and innovation, painting a wide and limitless picture of new possibilities—the sky is the limit. This Best Practice is about creating a positive environment for working relationships.

Red is the color of the heart. It is associated with the very core and being of something, and thus it has been **linked with Best Practice 3: Influencer of Inspiration and Leadership**™. This Best Practice is the heart of Legacy Leadership®. The Legacy Leader® influences, inspires and models excellence in leadership for everyone. This Best Practice is about making connections with individuals—the heart of relationships as well as leadership.

Green is the color of growth. Personal, professional and organizational growth is stimulated by drawing upon the strengths of others, which is the intent of **Best Practice 4: Advocator of Differences and Community**™. The Legacy Leader® intentionally recognizes differences as potential strengths and community growth stimulators. This Best Practice is about distinguishing individual strengths and inclusion of differing perspectives.

Purple is a color often associated with royalty, and royalty can imply authority—and accountability. A king's subjects are called upon to give account for their service under him. They are responsible to him. **Purple has been assigned to Best Practice 5: Calibrator of Responsibility and Accountability**™. We believe this is a noble Best Practice, and one most often misunderstood and neglected! This Best Practice is about execution and performance measured against vision and values.

We hope these colors will help bring the 5 Best Practices to mind for easy remembrance, and serve as a quick and efficient template for leadership behavior.

What Legacy Leaders® Need to:
Know, Believe and Do

BEST PRACTICE	Know **Essence:** Know that their role is to develop others, who develop others	Believe **Essence:** Believe that the major role of the leader is to see that others develop their full potential	Do **Essence:** Constantly see opportunities to develop people
Best Practice #1 **Holder of Vision and Values**™	o Know their own vision and values as a human being o Know who they are and purpose for being here. o Know and align with organizational goals	o Believe that without clear direction (from both vision and values) there is no leadership	o Develop and embody the vision/values that clearly establish direction
Best Practice #2 **Creator of Collaboration and Innovation**™	o Know how to listen and draw out what others don't know is within them. o Know they don't have to have the answers o Know that best group thinking is better than individual thinking o Know how to create an environment of trust	o Believe that better, newer creative/innovative solutions come from tapping the best thinking from everyone	o Create and sustain a trusting environment where it's okay to be brilliant as well as make mistakes.
Best Practice #3 **Influencer of Inspiration and Leadership**™	o Know that relationships are the fundamental building blocks of leadership o Know that everything they do and say influences others o Know what is inspiring to them personally o Know that in all times (good and bad) it takes courage to lead	o Believe that one must be inspired to inspire others o Believe that relationships are the heart of leadership	o Make sustainable relationships
Best Practice #4 **Advocator of Differences and Community**™	o Know that each and every person has a significant contribution to make o Know that people need community and to be acknowledged within it o Know that people work better from their strengths o Know that it may not be popular taking a stand for people. o Know that inclusive works better than exclusive	o Believe that everyone has a positive contribution to make o Believe that a Legacy Leader is a respecter of persons o Believe there is a richness in diversity of perspectives	o Discern differences/uniquenesses in perspective and strengths and utilize the differences in positive outcomes o Create synergistic relationships in teams and groups of stakeholders
Best Practice #5 **Calibrator of Responsibility and Accountability**™	o Know that they must execute against vision o Know that things are constantly changing and constant monitoring of trends and recalibration is necessary o Know that they must be personally responsible and accountable o Know that in order to gain commitment from workers, there must be clarity about expectations	o Believe that if people would keep their word, we could put our world (and our organizations) together better than they have ever been. o Believe that they are personally responsible for their sphere of influence	o Develop and execute against the vision and deliver on expectations through use of quality processes and methods o **Note: The "doing" part here is a 50,000' view. Refer to the LL Model.**

Using This Application Workbook

This book is designed to be used along with the book **"Legacy Leadership: The Leader's Guide to Lasting Greatness."** The model and concepts of Legacy Leadership are more fully explained there. This workbook contains only the bare minimum for understanding of Legacy Leadership. You may use this book with a coach or training facilitator, or on your own.

If you have had enough time to acquaint yourself with Legacy Leadership and the 5 Best Practices, as well as the associated Critical Success Skills, you may already know what areas you wish to focus on for your own personal and professional development. If so, you can attempt to complete the simple Development Plan on the next page, and work from there. This plan highlights only the strengths and challenges of each of the 5 Best Practices, and it is recommended that even if you wish to only target these areas, that you go ahead at some point and complete all the exercises for every best practice and every critical success skill. In this way you will be maximizing the potential this book has to launch you onto a path to greatness in your leadership.

For each Best Practice the associated self assessment page for that practice is included at the front of each best practice section. You may have already completed the Legacy Leadership Competency Inventory (LLCI), but if not, this is a great place to start. It will help you know your strengths and challenges in each practice area. Also, at the end of this workbook, a complete blank LLCI is offered so you can re-evaluate your competencies after your application exercises. You should see some huge improvements.

If you approach this workbook with a commitment to becoming a great leader, one who lives his or her legacy, you will appreciate the attention to details on each Best Practice and every one of the ten Critical Success Skills. Try not to skip over them. These are designed to bring you awareness of your own leadership, and help you improve dramatically, ready for any leadership challenge. This book is called a "journal" because if you approach these exercises with excitement for their potential in your leadership abilities, you will be doing a lot of writing. Don't skip over them. Put everything down you need to. If you have more to write than the space provided, use a supplemental journal. You will find over the years that follow, in your leadership journeys, this will become one of your most valuable tools.

Initial Development Plan

BEST PRACTICE	Top 3 Strengths in this Best Practice	Top 3 Challenges in this Best Practice (development opportunities)	Specific skills in this Best Practice I want to develop	My goals for development of this Best Practice
Holder of Vision and Values™	1. 2. 3.	1. 2. 3.		
Creator of Collaboration and Innovation™	1. 2. 3.	1. 2. 3.		
Influencer of Inspiration and Leadership™	1. 2. 3.	1. 2. 3.		
Advocator of Differences and Community™	1. 2. 3.	1. 2. 3.		
Calibrator of Responsibility and Accountability™	1. 2. 3.	1. 2. 3.		

NOTE: The Top 3 strengths, and the Top 3 Challenges are determined from your completed Legacy Leadership® Competency Inventory (LLCI). If you have not yet completed the inventory, you can still attempt to develop a plan for your studies based on what you already know about your leadership competencies now. Note, a full version of the LLCI is available at the end of this book.

NOTES

Best Practice 1
Holder of Vision and Values™

WHERE ARE YOU NOW?

The Legacy Leadership Competency Inventory (LLCI) is a good place to start your application journey. For each of the five Best Practices a rating page is provided so you can have a starting benchmark. The entire LLCI (with all 5 Best Practices) is also included at the back of this journal. You may wish to complete the assessment on the opposite page before beginning your journey, then the entire LLCI assessment again at the end where you will hopefully see vast improvement in your scores. The Self Assessment for Best Practice 1 in on the next page.

This competency inventory is an opportunity for leaders to receive information about their level of competency in each of the five practice contexts of Legacy Leadership. It provides a direction for learning, a guide for leader development and a model for developing leadership fully.

Instructions for Completion

For each Best Practice there is a set of ten descriptive statements. YOU ARE ASKED TO PROVIDE A RATING FOR **TWO QUESTIONS** FOR EACH STATEMENT (referred to as a "dual rating assessment"):

PERFORMANCE: How often **do I exhibit** this stated behavior/attitude?
EXPECTATIONS: How often is this stated behavior/attitude **expected to occur** in my position?

Read each statement carefully, and honestly rate yourself on a scale of 1 to 5 as follows:
- *This statement describes my actual current behavior/attitude (PERFORMANCE):*
- *The statement describes how often this behavior/attitude should occur (EXPECTATIONS):*
    1—Not At All
    2—Occasionally
    3—On Average
    4—Frequently
    5—Consistently

Rate yourself for BOTH Performance and Expectations using this scale.
After you have rated each statement, total each column under each of the two sets of responses (Performance and Expectations) and place the total score for each of the five columns in the blanks provided. Then add the column score total across from left to right for a total score for each set of ratings on each Best Practice. Graph your responses.

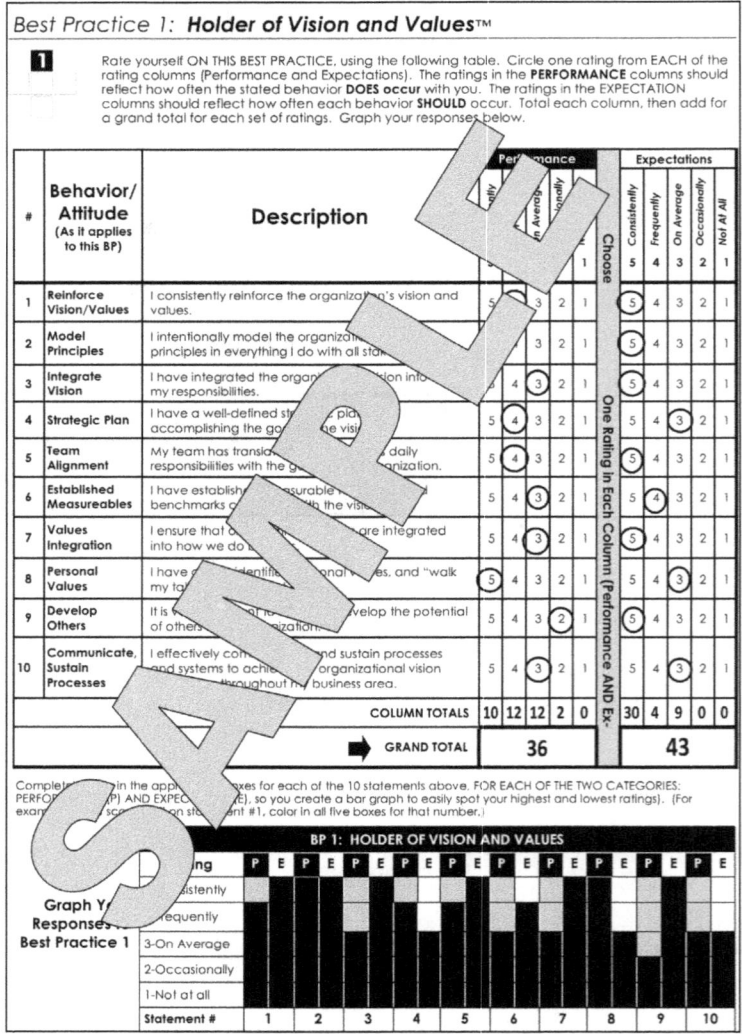

Best Practice 1: **Holder of Vision and Values**™

Rate yourself ON THIS BEST PRACTICE, using the following table. Circle one rating from EACH of the rating columns (Performance and Expectations). The ratings in the **PERFORMANCE** columns should reflect how often the stated behavior **DOES occur** with you. The ratings in the EXPECTATION columns should reflect how often each behavior **SHOULD** occur. Total each column, then add for a grand total for each set of ratings. Graph your responses below.

#	Behavior/Attitude (As it applies to this BP)	Description	Performance: Consistently 5	Frequently 4	On Average 3	Occasionally 2	Not At All 1		Expectations: Consistently 5	Frequently 4	On Average 3	Occasionally 2	Not At All 1
1	Reinforce Vision/Values	I consistently reinforce the organization's vision and values.	5	4	3	2	1	Choose One Rating in Each Column (Performance AND Expectations)	5	4	3	2	1
2	Model Principles	I intentionally model the organization's guiding principles in everything I do with all stakeholders.	5	4	3	2	1		5	4	3	2	1
3	Integrate Vision	I have integrated the organization's vision into all of my responsibilities.	5	4	3	2	1		5	4	3	2	1
4	Strategic Plan	I have a well-defined strategic plan for accomplishing the goals of the vision.	5	4	3	2	1		5	4	3	2	1
5	Team Alignment	My team has translated and aligned its daily responsibilities with the goals of the organization.	5	4	3	2	1		5	4	3	2	1
6	Established Measureables	I have established measurable milestones and benchmarks congruent with the vision.	5	4	3	2	1		5	4	3	2	1
7	Values Integration	I ensure that organizational values are integrated into how we do business.	5	4	3	2	1		5	4	3	2	1
8	Personal Values	I have clearly identified personal values, and "walk my talk" in everything I do.	5	4	3	2	1		5	4	3	2	1
9	Develop Others	It is very important to me that I develop the potential of others in the organization.	5	4	3	2	1		5	4	3	2	1
10	Communicate, Sustain Processes	I effectively communicate and sustain processes and systems to achieve the organizational vision and values throughout my business area.	5	4	3	2	1		5	4	3	2	1
		COLUMN TOTALS											
		➤ **GRAND TOTAL**											

Completely color in the appropriate boxes for each of the 10 statements above, FOR EACH OF THE TWO CATEGORIES: PERFORMANCE (P) AND EXPECTATION (E), so you create a bar graph to easily spot your highest and lowest ratings). (For example, if you scored "5" on statement #1, color in all five boxes for that number.)

Graph Your Responses to Best Practice 1

BP 1: HOLDER OF VISION AND VALUES™																				
Rating	P	E	P	E	P	E	P	E	P	E	P	E	P	E	P	E	P	E	P	E
5-Consistently																				
4-Frequently																				
3-On Average																				
2-Occasionally																				
1-Not at all																				
Statement #	1		2		3		4		5		6		7		8		9		10	

APPLY THE BASICS

Critical Success Skills: Core Competencies

Holding Vision and Values involves an unswerving commitment to intentional behavior that enables an organization to realize its vision and operate with integrity—consistently. These behaviors are not mere references to non-measurable goals or giving lip service to a stated code of ethics. A Legacy Leader embraces and practices ten critical success skills which serve to shift entire organizational cultures to realize goals, and doing so also provides a solid leadership model for tomorrow's leaders.

The success skills for this first Legacy Practice will always be hallmarks of great leaders.

1. Consistently reinforce organizational vision and values.
2. Intentionally model guiding principles in everything, with everyone.
3. Personally integrate organization's vision in all responsibilities.
4. Have a well-defined strategic plan for accomplishing the vision.
5. Enable the team to translate organizational vision, and align daily responsibilities with organizational goals.
6. Establish measurable milestones congruent with vision.
7. Ensure that organizational values are integrated into how the organization does business.
8. Clearly identify your personal values; "walk the talk" in everything.
9. Place importance on developing others.
10. Effectively communicate, sustain processes to achieve vision and values.

Essence: *Being* a Legacy Leader
The BE-Attitudes of a Holder of Vision and Values

When we attempt to compile lists of the necessary attitudes and qualities of good leaders as they might pertain to this Legacy Practice, we would expect to see such core characteristics as visionary, a communicator, open and not guarded, a role model, and a person of integrity. These would head the list of many other attitudes that could be named here. However, this book is not about just good, or great, leaders. It is about *Legacy* Leaders. Legacy sets these leaders apart from all others. Leaders who live their legacy now will possess certain fundamental attributes and inclinations that enable them to truly lead for legacy as they hold vision and values. We have identified five specific foundational attitudes that distinguish *Legacy* Leaders in this Legacy Practice. These are not listed in any order of importance. Brief descriptions of the top five follow. *A Legacy Leader, a Holder of Vision and Values, IS:*

1. **Others-Oriented**
This person conducts him or herself in ways that benefit others first, not self. These leaders are aware of other people, their roles, their performance and their needs, and always seek to lift others before self. This leader is sensitive to development opportunities for others. Legacy Leaders are aware of how their personal behavior affects other people and seek to either maximize the positive impact, or minimize the negative.

☐ **Others-Oriented**
☐ **Guardian**
☐ **Seamless**
☐ **Values-Driven**
☐ **Whole Systems Thinker**

2. **A Guardian**
This person always protects and champions what is important, such as vision and values, guarding them against erosion or loss, and seeking their incorporation into all behavior and processes.

3. **Seamless**
This person's life and behavior looks the same regardless of position, place or politics. Business conduct is the same as personal conduct. Public behavior is the same as private behavior. Others cannot detect a change in behavior depending on situation or circumstances.

4. **Values-Driven**
This person does everything, in all places and positions, based on a personal and professional set of values. These values drive and shape all behavior. This leader is also constantly measuring behavior against values, making correction or changes as necessary.

5. **A Whole Systems Thinker**
This person has the ability to see life around him or her as a whole system with many parts. This is true in business and general life. These leaders are able to grasp the "big picture" but also understand the many parts that make up that picture. They see the inter-relationships among the parts and how all contribute to the whole.

BE-ATTITUDE SELF ASSESSMENT

How developed is your core being for becoming a Legacy Leader in this Legacy Practice? After reading the descriptions of these BE-Attitudes above, rate yourself *(circle one)* on the following scale, then go on to the steps and questions that follow.

	BE-ATTITUDES of a Holder of Vision and Values	RATING: 5=all the time, 0=not at all					
1	I am others-oriented.	5	4	3	2	1	0
2	I am a guardian of what is important.	5	4	3	2	1	0
3	I am seamless in my behavior in all places.	5	4	3	2	1	0
4	I am values-driven.	5	4	3	2	1	0
5	I am a whole systems thinker.	5	4	3	2	1	0

Where do your ratings fall? How many 5's? Any 2's or below? Any zeros? Here are some suggestions for building the core being of a *legacy* Holder of Vision and Values.

1. ***Choose your two highest ratings***. Determine how you can leverage these strengths to be even more effective in developing and living your leadership legacy. ***Also choose two of your lowest*** rating attitudes to be your "work on" areas for improvement. Use the questions below to build your BE-attitudes.

2. ***Think of someone you know to be this***, to have this attitude, for each of the two areas you selected for improvement. For example, if you scored yourself low in being seamless in your behavior in all places, who do you know whose behavior *is* seamless (past or present)? Identify one person for each of the areas you want to develop and do the following exercises. Write the attitudes and person's name in the space provided:

	BE- ATTITUDE	Person I know who displays this be-attitude
1		
2		

Consider the following for each attitude, and person listed:

a. What does this person do that lets me, and others, know he or she is _____ (BE-Attitude)?

b. How can I emulate this behavior/attitude?

c. How will this behavior help me become a better leader? A Legacy Leader?

3. After completing the above steps, **_make a commitment_** to improve. Choose one of your "work on" attitudes each week, and focus on improving that attitude in all you think, do and speak.

    a. Be aware of your behavior and thought processes during the week, as they pertain to that attitude.

    b. Create a mental reminder that will alert you to old behavior and thought patterns you want to change.

    c. When you are alerted to old behavior and thought patterns, change them immediately, if possible. If not, use that experience to help remind you in the future. Consider what triggered this old behavior or attitude, and how you can respond differently in the future.

    d. Evaluate your week for progress and determine how you can improve next week.

    e. The following week, add another "work on" attitude as your focus, without neglecting the first one.

    f. Keep doing this until you notice a definite change (improvement), so that your improved attitude has become part of you, part of your core being as a Legacy Leader. Chances are if *you* notice an improvement, others will as well.

    g. If journaling is familiar and comfortable for you, consider keeping track of your BE-Attitude development. Brush away discouragement if things don't change immediately. They will, especially if this is the way you want to be. Sometimes we just need to rethink or reframe how we think and do.

WRITE ANY COMMENTS BELOW YOU THINK MIGHT HELP YOU STRENGTHEN THESE BE-ATTITUDES...

NOTES

DRILL DOWNS
Best Practice 1

The following section includes drill down *(more targeted and focused)* opportunities for each of the ten critical success skills for Best Practice 1. You may wish to complete the ones you have determined you need to strengthen first, but in order to truly round out your competencies and skills in this best practice, it is best to complete them all.

Drill Down 1:1

Best Practice 1:1

Holder of Vision and Values™

CRITICAL SUCCESS SKILL #1:

Consistently reinforce the organization's vision and values.

Vision

Does your organization have a stated vision? You might be surprised how many do not. Does every member of your team know, understand and have commitment to this vision? If you cannot answer a solid YES to these questions, it might be time to gather the executive team together and develop a vision that will drive your organization, and be sure every member of the organization knows it. If you do have an established organizational vision, consider these questions:

- How can you, and how do you, reinforce the organization's vision on a daily basis within your functional area?

- How can you hold yourself accountable for this behavior?

Something to Think About...

"A lasting, powerful vision has two components: a core ideology and an envisioned future. Core ideology itself has two parts: core values (guiding principles by which your company navigates) and core purpose (an organization's most fundamental reason for being and what motivates people to do the company's work)."
—*Excerpt from "Building Your Company's Vision" by James C. Collins and Jerry I. Porras*

Does your organizational vision statement provide you with clarity and guidance at critical decision points?

ANSWERS

Values

The same questions stated above for vision apply for values. Does your organization have a set of Guiding Principles (values)? Does every member of your team know, understand and have commitment to these Guiding Principles? If not, consider a collaborative effort to draft such a set of values that will serve as a navigational beacon for your organization. If you do have established values (a written set of Guiding Principles), consider these questions:

- How can you reinforce the values of this organization, and your personal values, in a practical day-to-day manner within your functional area?

- What evidence of this do you see?

1:1 continued

TOP THREE

List your top 3 learnings, top 3 action plans, or top 3 personal reminders regarding this Critical Success Skill.

Drill Down 1:2

Best Practice 1:2

Holder of Vision and Values™

CRITICAL SUCCESS SKILL #2:
Intentionally model guiding principles in everything, with everyone.

The Keys

In the CSS listed above, there are three key words to understanding and implementing this skill:

INTENTIONALLY	MODEL	ALL/EVERYTHING
With purpose, firmly and with steadfastness; with sharply focused design.	To serve as an example, to display, to show what is typical, natural, desired	These words have the same meaning: nothing and no one excluded. All inclusive.

- With the definitions above in mind, and your organization's Guiding Principles, what must **you** do in order to successfully implement this Critical Success Skill in your area of responsibility? *(It is very easy to state values in writing, and quite another thing to actually live them.)*

Something to Think About...

"Eighty percent of Fortune 500 companies promote their values publicly. Here's one set from 2000: 'Communication, Respect, Integrity, Excellence.' Recognize the company? It's Enron, of course!... Once values have been developed, then they need to be inserted into every employee-related process, from hiring, performance management, rewards systems, to dismissal policies...You can create company values that reflect the true nature of your organization...and if properly implemented, they ought to ensure that your company doesn't suffer the fate of Enron."
—*Excerpt from "Make Your Values Mean Something" by Patrick M. Lencioni Harvard Business Review*

Do the guiding principles reflect the true nature of your organization? How can you ensure they are properly implemented?

ANSWERS

- Does every member of your team, all stakeholders, have knowledge and understanding of these organizational Guiding Principles? How do these GPs affect your and their behavior?

- What is the result of abiding by them—or not?

- What area-wide accountabilities are in place?

1:2 continued

TOP THREE

List your top 3 learnings, top 3 action plans, or top 3 personal reminders regarding this Critical Success Skill.

Drill Down 1:3

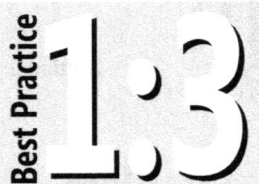

Best Practice 1:3

CRITICAL SUCCESS SKILL #3:
Integrate the organization's vision into all areas of responsibility.

Holder of Vision and Values™

Something to Think About...

"Any successful journey of continual improvement shows five components: a vision of a desired end state; knowledge of where we are now, our present state; a road map for strategic intent; an internal drive system; a value system of principles."
—Robert R. Thompson

Best Practice 1 is about Vision and Values. The "bookend" to this is Best Practice 5, about Responsibility and Accountability. How does the statement above apply to these two Best Practices of Legacy Leadership®? How does this help integrate the organizational vision? What commitment will you make?

Integrating the Organization's Vision

Reinforcing
In the last Drill Down the concept of **reinforcing** the vision was highlighted. Reinforcing is about strengthening.

Disseminating
In the article "Waking Up IBM" (Harvard Business Review) G. Hamel stated: *"The vision must be **disseminated** if it is to inspire change and attract others to the cause."* Disseminating is about spreading and broadcasting—getting the word out.

Implementing
In the Ivey Business Journal, E. Beaudan said: **"Leadership is not only about creating vision and excitement and moving the organization forward during change, it is about managing change and strategy in a way that focuses people's attention on the dynamics of implementation. Leaders need to balance their involvement in creating strategy with the more demanding task of working their way through the clarification and engagement process."** Implementation is about fulfilling and carrying out.

ANSWERS

A vision is not just a set of written words, disseminated for knowledge and reinforced for strength. After the vision is drafted, disseminated and reinforced, there is a critical action required before any fulfillment can be realized—**integration**. **Integration is about bringing together, incorporating into a unified, harmonious whole.**

- Think about the word "integration." How can you integrate the organization's vision into your area of responsibility to where it is obvious by your actions and behavior?

- What changes or commitments will you have to make in order to do this?

- Is the organization's vision reflected in your personal goals? How?

1:3 continued

TOP THREE

List your top 3 learnings, top 3 action plans, or top 3 personal reminders regarding this Critical Success Skill.

Drill Down 1:4

Best Practice 1:4

CRITICAL SUCCESS SKILL #4:
Have a well-defined strategic plan for accomplishing the goals of the vision.

Holder of Vision and Values™

Accomplishing the Organizational Vision with Strategic Planning

We have already discussed the reinforcing and integrating of vision. In order to do either of these effectively, it is vital to have a strategic plan. Harvey Mackay said, **"A dream is just a dream. A goal is a dream with a plan and a deadline."** So it is with vision.

"Organizations need tools for communicating both their strategy and the processes and systems that will help them implement that strategy. Strategy maps provide such a tool because they give employees a clear line of sight into how their jobs are linked to the overall objectives of the organization, enabling them to work in a coordinated, collaborative fashion toward the next company's desired goals. The best way to build strategy maps is from the top down, starting with the destination and then charting the routes that will lead there."

From "Having Trouble With Your Strategy? Then Map It"
Kaplan, R.S. & Norton, D.P.
Harvard Business Journal

It is clear that vision must be teamed with strategy.

Something to Think About...

Carl Honoré interviewed one of the world's leading management thinkers, Charles Handy, on his views on leadership. Handy believes that the ideal leader is passionate and someone who can combine a strategic sense with a well-defined vision. For him, vision and strategy are two sides of the same coin.

C. Honoré
"Charles Handy: An Inventive Mind, Part Two"
Ivey Business Journal

Have you developed an operational strategy for your functional area that has a line of sight directly to the organization's vision? If so, what is it?

★ ANSWERS

- Make a list of concrete steps which will form the basic outline of your strategic plan to accomplish the organizational vision for your area of responsibility. Outline at least 7 steps, and consider your previous thinking about reinforcing and integrating the vision. *(If your organization has an existing written strategic plan, capture the outline in basic bullet points here. What in particular relates to your area of responsibility?)*

1:4
continued

TOP THREE

List your top 3 learnings, top 3 action plans, or top 3 personal reminders regarding this Critical Success Skill.

Drill Down 1:5

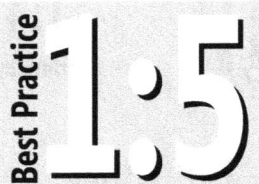

Best Practice 1:5

CRITICAL SUCCESS SKILL #5:
Teams have translated and aligned daily responsibilities with the goals of the organization.

Holder of Vision and Values™

Team Translation and Alignment with the Organizational Vision

The organization's vision and your strategic plan to accomplish it don't stop with you. They must be "broadcast" to your entire team. Clear communication is essential, but this is only the beginning.

- Using the strategy you developed in the previous Drill Down (or existing corporate strategic plan), how will you help your team translate the organization's vision for applicability in your area of responsibility? List practical steps.

Something to Think About...

"I believe that you get greater effectiveness in your work when you tie people's personal mission with the corporate mission."
—Richard Barrett

Organizational and personal mission can be similar to vision, though not exactly the same. Substitute the organization's vision for the word "mission" in the above quote. Is what this person suggests possible? How? How would you tie the organizational vision to the personal vision of your team members?

ANSWERS

- Benjamin Disraeli said, *"The secret of success is constancy of purpose."* How does this relate to translating and aligning the organization's vision with daily area responsibilities?

- What will be your "constancy of purpose" (from quote above) and how will you be sure it is aligned with the company's strategic plan—consistently?

1:5 continued

TOP THREE

List your top 3 learnings, top 3 action plans, or top 3 personal reminders regarding this Critical Success Skill.

Drill Down 1:6

Best Practice 1:6

CRITICAL SUCCESS SKILL #6:
Have established measurable milestones and benchmarks congruent with the vision.

Holder of Vision and Values™

Measurable Milestones and Benchmarks

You know the vision. You have a strategic plan. You have communicated clearly and helped your team translate the vision and align it with daily responsibilities. Now what? How will you know if you are successfully accomplishing the vision? The next step is setting the standards, identifying the measurable milestones and benchmarks that will serve as your guide on the path to successfully accomplishing your organizational vision.

Without the measurement markers, you and your team have no way of knowing concretely if your work has accomplished the vision. Peter Drucker said, *"If you can't measure it, you can't manage it."* It's that simple.

Something to Think About...

"Visioning does not mean soft and undisciplined. Quite the contrary. Visionary companies have such clarity about who they are, what they're all about, and what they're trying to achieve, they tend not to have much room for people unwilling or unsuited to their demanding standards."
—*James Collins*

We have already seen how vision must be wed to strategy. Strategy must be measured with standards. Do you agree with the above quotation? What does this mean for you, the leader, in your area of responsibility?

ANSWERS

- List <u>at least</u> 5 different key performance indicators, along with timelines or due dates that you and your team will use to confirm that you are, or take actions when you are not, accomplishing the vision and strategy in your respective areas of responsibility.

- How often and in what manner will you measure your success against these markers? How will you correct any misalignment? Try to be specific here, and develop a policy and procedures that can be consistently followed. What are areas of responsibility and accountability for these tasks?

1:6
continued

TOP THREE

List your top 3 learnings, top 3 action plans, or top 3 personal reminders regarding this Critical Success Skill.

Drill Down 1:7

Best Practice 1:7

Holder of Vision and Values™

CRITICAL SUCCESS SKILL #7:
Ensure that organizational values are integrated into how you do business.

Integrating Guiding Principles

Drill Down 1:2 (BP1-CSS2) discussed the keys for intentionally modeling Guiding Principles. Modeling is the beginning of integrating. This Critical Success Skill is about ENSURING that these values and principles are an integrated part of how you do business.

- What does the complete integration of Guiding Principles look like in your area of responsibility? What are the signs of integration, and the signs of non-integration?

Something to Think About...

"Preach what you practice. It's not enough to have the right values. You must clarify them and hammer them home to customers, employees, suppliers, and shareholders through your words and deeds."
—From "Lead for Loyalty"
Frederick F. Reichheld
Harvard Business Review

Modeling Guiding Principles within the organization may not be enough. How does the quotation above relate to complete integration of those values? How will you do this?

ANSWERS

- What steps would you need to take in order to ENSURE integration?

1:7
continued

TOP THREE

List your top 3 learnings, top 3 action plans, or top 3 personal reminders regarding this Critical Success Skill.

- What will you do should you determine that the organization's Guiding Principles have not been integrated, or are not being modeled throughout your area of responsibility? It is always helpful to plan ahead the actions you will take in this event. How will you address this issue with your team members, and how will you set accountability in place for this?

Drill Down 1:8

Best Practice 1:8

CRITICAL SUCCESS SKILL #8:
Have clearly identified personal values, and "walk the talk" in everything you do.

Holder of Vision and Values™

"Walking the Talk" of Clearly Identified Personal Values

All of your behavior is driven by your personal values set, whether you are aware of it or not. This set of values is comprised of what you consider true, valid and important about three main areas of your life: PERSONAL, BUSINESS (PROFESSIONAL), and SPIRITUAL.

Don Meyer said *"It is always easy to do right when you know ahead of time what you stand for."* Most people assume they already have a set of clearly defined values, but may not have taken the time to delineate and clarify them in order to know how they will respond in certain situations.

Something to Think About...

"People can't live with change if there's not a changeless core inside them. The key to the ability to change is a changeless sense of who you are, what you are about and what you value."
—From <u>The Seven Habits of Highly Effective People</u> By Stephen R. Covey

Why is it important for you, and your team members, to have clearly identified personal values, AND to always work in alignment with those values, especially as they relate to your work in this organization?

- List at least 5 core values in your **PERSONAL** life:

ANSWERS

- List at least 5 core values in your **PROFESSIONAL** life:

- List at least 5 core values in your **SPIRITUAL** life:

- What do you need to do in order to consistently "walk the talk" of your above stated values? How will you handle potential "conflicts" in your work in this organization?

1:8
continued

TOP THREE

List your top 3 learnings, top 3 action plans, or top 3 personal reminders regarding this Critical Success Skill.

BENEFITS OF RECOGNIZING YOUR VALUES
- Solidify your guiding principles
- Be congruent and consistent
- Be intentional about your leadership
- Determine alignment (or lack of alignment) with organizational values
- Honesty in all behavior
- Be your real self
- Have a solid foundation for all decisions and actions

Drill Down 1:9

Best Practice 1:9

CRITICAL SUCCESS SKILL #9:
It is important (to you) that you develop the potential of others in the organization.

Holder of Vision and Values™

Developing Others

Developing others, working at discovering the potential leadership qualities of your team members, is essential to the organizational vision. This is part of what makes a good leader great, and is the whole purpose behind the concept of LEGACY. Not everyone may possess the skills, abilities and potential to be a great leader, but everyone will benefit from someone intentionally working to develop that person's potential.

- On a scale of 1 to 5 (5 being the highest) rate yourself as a **LEGACY** Leader, one who intentionally develops the potential of others, at this moment.

    RATING:_____

- If you scored yourself a 3 or below, what can you do to bring your rating up to a 5, with your current team members? List practical steps.

Something to Think About...

"While great leaders may be as rare as great runners, great actors, or great painters, everyone has leadership potential, just as everyone has some ability at running, acting, and painting."

—Warren G. Bennis and Burt Nanus

Do you believe this quotation? How will knowing this affect how you relate and work with your team members? What does this have to do with the organization's vision?

ANSWERS

- Write down the names of your team members and then one or two words for each that signifies the potential you see in each. Then write at least 2 practical things **you will do to** encourage that potential.

Name	Potential	How I Will Encourage Development

1:9 continued

TOP THREE

List your top 3 learnings, top 3 action plans, or top 3 personal reminders regarding this Critical Success Skill.

Drill Down 1:10

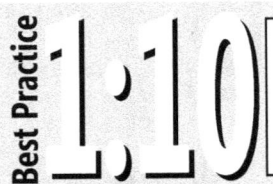

Best Practice 1:10

CRITICAL SUCCESS SKILL #10:
Effectively communicate and sustain processes and systems to achieve the organizational vision and values throughout your business area.

Holder of Vision and Values™

Something to Think About...

"An essential part of being a leader is being a good teacher. Good teaching is universal, whatever the topic....

**Point # 6:
Keep it clear if you can't keep it simple. The essence of teaching is communication."**

From "Attention Class!!!
16 Ways to be a
SmarterTeacher"
By Chuck Salter
Fast Company

*As a leader, are you a good teacher?
Is your communication clear AND simple?*

Sustaining Processes and Systems to Achieve Vision and Values

This is the last of the 10 Critical Success Skills for Best Practice 1: Holder of Vision and Values™. It's also the bottom line. You are the boss in your area of responsibility. Ultimately, it is your job to effectively communicate, then sustain, all the processes and systems of your area in order to achieve the goals of the vision and the core values of the Guiding Principles. After working through these last Drill Downs, you should be getting a much better idea of what it means to HOLD vision and values.

- Based solely upon what you see as responses from your team members *(not on your personal opinion),* how effective is your communication in this regard? What practical steps can you take to improve it?

ANSWERS

- Are you consistently successful in sustaining all processes and systems in your area of responsibility, and can you honestly say your area has accomplished the organization's vision and achieved its values? If not, why not? What practical steps can you take to move closer to this goal?

- What is the essence of what you have learned about being a HOLDER of Vision and Values™? How are you implementing this?

1:10 continued

TOP THREE

List your top 3 learnings, top 3 action plans, or top 3 personal reminders regarding this Critical Success Skill.

Developing Personal Vision

Write Your Personal Vision Statement

Vision means you have an inner calling, something within that needs to be intentionally identified and stated. It defines how we combine our strengths, our needs and our intentions with enjoyable and fulfilling pursuits. A very brief example of a personal vision statement is "To serve as a catalyst revolutionizing the lives of individuals and their companies." Generally, a personal vision statement will actually include several statements that, taken together, become a singular statement about that person's goals, aims, ambitions, capabilities, beliefs, and desires. To be representative of the person, however, it must be written with all their strengths, needs and intentions in mind.

Developing this personal vision statement requires thoughtful reflection. Consider the following as you develop your statement:

- **The big picture of your life**
- **The things you find most enjoyable**
- **Your strengths**
- **Your needs**
- **Your intentions for life**
- **Your life goals**
- **Your career goals**
- **Where you find significance, fulfillment, passion**
- **Your internal wants and desires (other than material things)**
- **Your wants for others**
- **Your values and beliefs**

After giving careful thought to the above considerations, develop a series of statements using this pattern:

- **ACTION**
  (use a verb to denote what you will DO)

- **OBJECTIVE**
  (the value or aim of the action)

- **WITH WHAT OR WHOM**
  (the thing, person, group of importance to you)

(see next page for exercise)

Your Personal Vision Statement

SAMPLE—
My vision is:

To create
    ACTION (use a verb to denote what you will DO)

positive environments
    OBJECTIVE (the value or aim of the action)

for shifts in individuals or organizations I lead.
    WITH WHAT OR WHOM (the thing, person, group of importance to you)

Vision Statement:
My vision is to create positive environments for shifts in individuals or organizations I lead.

My Personal Vision Statement

If necessary, write as many statements as you need to identify your vision.

Write these statements here: **My vision is....**

1.

2.

3.

4.

5.

6.

7.

8.

9.

10.

Now here's a real challenge. Can you write a single statement that encompasses all of the above into one comprehensive personal vision statement? Think about it carefully. If you could express your entire vision in one sentence, how would you write it?

Do it here....

Developing Values

Spend some time looking at these PERSONAL-PROFESSIONAL-SPIRITUAL values and determine which are of highest value to you. Rank them from 1 (lowest value) to 5 (highest value). Continued on next page.

#	VALUE	1	2	3	4	5	COMMENT
WHAT IS OF PERSONAL VALUE TO YOU?							
1	Knowledge of self						
2	Being "together"						
3	Congruent life in all areas						
4	Continued life education						
5	Balanced life						
6	Excellent physical health						
7	Being in control						
8	Personal development						
9	Financial wealth						
10	Positive attitude						
11	Stroked ego						
12	High self-esteem						
13	Personal grooming						
14	Serving others						
15	High energy						
16	Well educated						
17	Personal integrity						
18	Open minded/accepting						
19	Pleasant surroundings						
20	Good relationships						
21							
22							
WHAT IS OF PROFESSIONAL VALUE TO YOU?							
1	Making it to the "top"						
2	Great network						
3	Serving others						
4	Making lots of money						
5	Integrity						
6	Good working relationships						
7	Doing my best						
8	Always learning, developing						
9	Pleasant environment						
10	Being happy at work						
11	Being a leader						
12	Organization						
13	Being focused						
14	Being in control						
15	Fitting in						
16	Adaptive and flexible						
17	Being right						
18	Collaboration						
19	Ethics						
20	Acknowledgement/reward						
21							
22							

#	VALUE	1	2	3	4	5	COMMENT
	WHAT IS OF SPIRITUAL VALUE TO YOU?						
1	Having a faith						
2	Knowing about my faith						
3	Living my faith						
4	Continued faith learning						
5	Sharing my faith						
6	Submission to my faith						
7	Being with others of my faith						
8	Understanding my faith						
9	My spiritual future						
10	Spiritual failure of others						
11	Respect for faith of others						
12	Spiritual relationships						
13	Faith-shaped values						
14	Faith values obvious in all areas of my life						
15	Faith integrity (actions match beliefs)						
16	Positive spiritual attitude						
17	Rewarding spiritual life						
18	Faith as foundation for all other activities						
19	Faith as basis for priorities						
20	Contentment with my faith						
21							
22							

Think About This…

1. Where are your "5" responses? What items listed here did you find most valuable to you? Can you comment on why this is so?

2. Did any of your responses surprise you (including your personalized fill-in blanks)? Why?

3. Do you notice any "clustering" of values? That is, certain related items all scoring high or low marks? If so, what and why? *(for example, you scored 5s on items all related to sharing, or all related to contentment, or all related to self-esteem, etc.)*

Corporate Values

As a personal or organizational exercise, begin to list (and then add as you think of more) values which you know to be those of your organization, or those you would want to be held by an organization for which you worked. Depending on your situation, you may wish to share this list with others on your team and within your organization as a tool to gain clarity and understanding around your organization's values. If you are not working within an organization at this time, you might choose to use this list as a reference guide for any organization you might serve in the future, or to help clients or others develop their own corporate values.

RANK	CORPORATE VALUE	RANK	CORPORATE VALUE

Best Practice 1

Holder of Vision and Values™

Best Practice 1 Application Notes

Legacy Leadership Application Workbook

Best Practice 2
Creator of Collaboration and Innovation™

WHERE ARE YOU NOW?

Take a current snapshot of your leadership skills and competencies for this Best Practice right now. A sample scoring sheet is shown below. The assessment for BP2 is found on the next page.

Instructions for Completion

For each Best Practice there is a set of ten descriptive statements. YOU ARE ASKED TO PROVIDE A RATING FOR **TWO QUESTIONS** FOR EACH STATEMENT (referred to as a "dual rating assessment"):

PERFORMANCE: How often **do I exhibit** this stated behavior/attitude?
EXPECTATIONS: How often is this stated behavior/attitude **expected to occur** in my position?

Read each statement carefully, and honestly rate yourself on a scale of 1 to 5 as follows:
- *This statement describes my actual current behavior/attitude (PERFORMANCE):*
- *The statement describes how often this behavior/attitude should occur (EXPECTATIONS):*
    1—Not At All
    2—Occasionally
    3—On Average
    4—Frequently
    5—Consistently

Rate yourself for BOTH Performance and Expectations using this scale.

After you have rated each statement, total each column under each of the two sets of responses (Performance and Expectations) and place the total score for each of the five columns in the blanks provided. Then add the column score total across from left to right for a total score for each set of ratings on each Best Practice. Graph your responses.

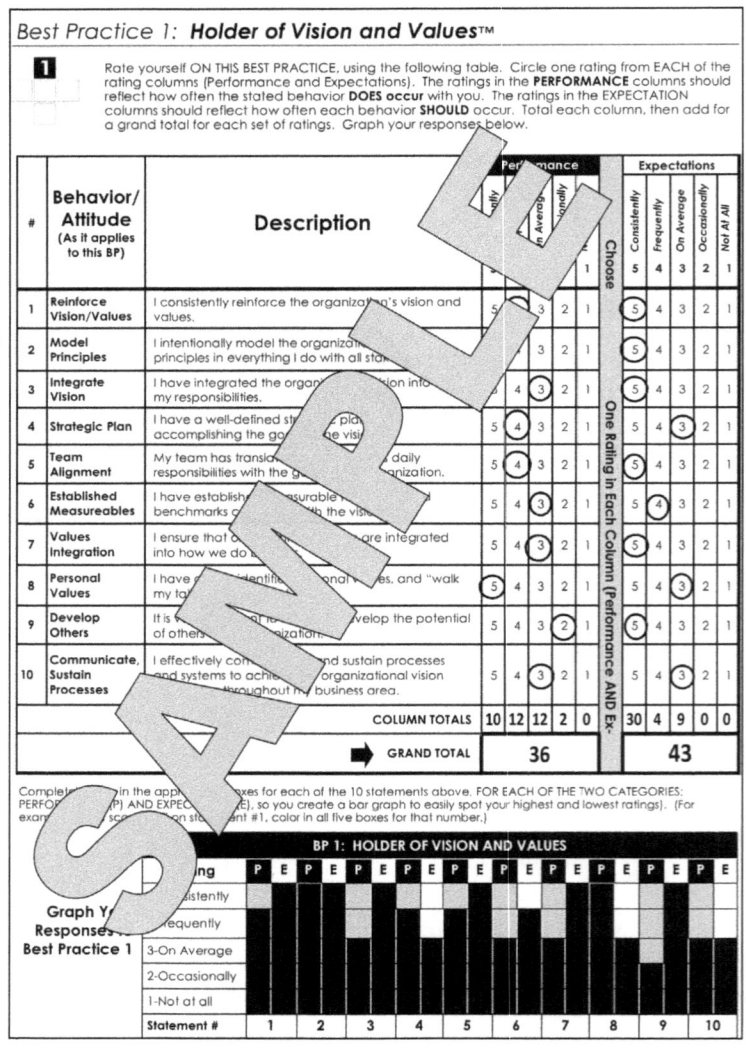

Legacy Leadership Application Workbook

Best Practice 2: **Creator of Collaboration and Innovation**™

Rate yourself ON THIS BEST PRACTICE, using the following table. Circle one rating from EACH of the rating columns (Performance and Expectations). The ratings in the **PERFORMANCE** columns should reflect how often the stated behavior **DOES occur** with you. The ratings in the EXPECTATION columns should reflect how often each behavior **SHOULD** occur. Total each column, then add for a grand total for each set of ratings. Graph your responses below.

#	Behavior/Attitude (As it applies to this BP)	Description	Performance — Consistently 5	Frequently 4	On Average 3	Occasionally 2	Not At All 1		Expectations — Consistently 5	Frequently 4	On Average 3	Occasionally 2	Not At All 1
1	Innovative Possibilities	I create possibilities that are both innovative and sound for the organization.	5	4	3	2	1	Choose One Rating in Each Column (Performance AND Expectations)	5	4	3	2	1
2	Trusting Environment	I foster a learning, trusting environment where true collaboration and innovation are unleashed.	5	4	3	2	1		5	4	3	2	1
3	Masterful Listener	I am a masterful listener for both what is said and what is not said.	5	4	3	2	1		5	4	3	2	1
4	Comfortable Learning from	I am comfortable not knowing "the answers" and learning from individual perspectives.	5	4	3	2	1		5	4	3	2	1
5	Opportunities in Disagreement	I draw out differing perspectives and believe that disagreement is a learning opportunity.	5	4	3	2	1		5	4	3	2	1
6	Timely Questioning	I keep in mind the bigger picture while asking timely, tough questions.	5	4	3	2	1		5	4	3	2	1
7	Innovate for Future	I set the tone for thinking beyond where we are presently in order to innovate now for the future.	5	4	3	2	1		5	4	3	2	1
8	Organizational, Marketplace Projection	I can project how ideas may play out in the organization and marketplace.	5	4	3	2	1		5	4	3	2	1
9	Discern need (or not) for Change	I can discern, and assist others to understand, when change needs to occur and when it does not.	5	4	3	2	1		5	4	3	2	1
10	Facilitate Best Group Thinking	I am a masterful facilitator of conversations such that everyone contributes their best thinking toward the task/issue at hand.	5	4	3	2	1		5	4	3	2	1
		COLUMN TOTALS											
		➤ **GRAND TOTAL**											

Completely color in the appropriate boxes for each of the 10 statements above, FOR EACH OF THE TWO CATEGORIES: PERFORMANCE (P) AND EXPECTATION (E), so you create a bar graph to easily spot your highest and lowest ratings). (For example, if you scored "5" on statement #1, color in all five boxes for that number.)

Graph Your Responses to Best Practice 2

BP 2: CREATOR OF COLLABORATION AND INNOVATION™																					
Rating	P	E	P	E	P	E	P	E	P	E	P	E	P	E	P	E	P	E	P	E
5-Consistently																				
4-Frequently																				
3-On Average																				
2-Occasionally																				
1-Not at all																				
Statement #	1		2		3		4		5		6		7		8		9		10	

© 2017-2021. CoachWorks® International, Inc. Dallas, TX. All International Rights Reserved. Do not duplicate.

APPLY THE BASICS

Critical Success Skills: Core Competencies

The ten critical success skills that build legacy around Best Practice 2 involve certain behaviors that advance the mere concepts of collaboration and innovation to the place where the leader is responsible for actively and intentionally creating these opportunities. To create *collaboration* within an organization, the Legacy Leader ensures high levels of trust, develops processes for building and capturing the collaboration, and encourages a team spirit. Creating *innovation* relies first on the collaborative process, then on a creative environment that challenges new thought, without boundaries.

1. Create innovative and sound possibilities for the organization.
2. Foster a learning, trusting environment for true collaboration and innovation.
3. Masterfully listen for both what is said and not said.
4. Be comfortable not knowing "the answers" and learn from individual perspectives.
5. Draw out differing perspectives and believe disagreement is a learning opportunity.
6. Ask timely, tough questions while keeping in mind the big picture.
7. Set the tone for thinking beyond the present in order to innovate for the future.
8. Project how ideas will play out in the organization and in the marketplace.
9. Discern, and assist others to understand, when change needs to happen and when not.
10. Masterfully facilitate conversations so everyone contributes best thinking toward task/goal.

Essence: *Being* a Legacy Leader
The BE-Attitudes of a Creator of Collaboration and Innovation

There are many attitudes and core characteristics necessary for all good leaders. For this Legacy Practice, those might include: trustworthy, affirming, sharing, creative, observant, and collaborative, among many others we could list here. To achieve greatness, however, a Legacy Leader takes core attitudes to a higher level—more focused, purposeful and conscious, until they are integrated into who this leader is, every day in every place. We have listed attitudes, or qualities, that we consider the Top Five BE-attitudes for your consideration in this Legacy Practice. These are not listed in any order of importance. Brief descriptions follow.
A Legacy Leader, a Creator of Collaboration and Innovation, IS:

1. A Trust Builder
This person always seeks to build trust in relationships. It is an automatic inclination which is composed of and driven by both trustworthiness and a trusting nature. These people have a mind set of connectiveness, and know that trust is built in order to connect firmly with others.

2. **An Intuitive Listener**
Listening is a core quality for this person, but it is also accompanied with an intuitive and discerning ear. This person desires to hear others, and consciously listens both to what is said, and what is not said. This person can gather an amazing amount of information by listening well and often.

☐ A Trust Builder
☐ An Intuitive Listener
☐ Possibility Minded
☐ "Charge-Neutral"
☐ Mentally Agile

3. **Possibility-Minded**
This person has developed an automatic reflex which allows them to see possibilities and opportunities, even when others may not. He or she is open-minded, and is able do mental feasibility exercises in almost any situation. This person is approachable, open to innovative thinking, and can thoroughly consider potential favorable possibilities in almost any situation.

4. **Charge-Neutral**
This is a term used in training coaches to be unbiased, non-judgmental and non-positioned with clients. A person who is charge-neutral has a neutral starting point for all ideas, people and things. This person does not pre-judge anything or anyone, and is open to receive all information (uncensored) before making decisions or judgments.

5. **Mentally Agile**
This characteristic is not necessarily a function of intelligence, but the ability to think quickly, remain flexible, shift gears as necessary and allow the ebb and flow of ideas to chart courses. This person has the ability to weigh ideas and actions quickly, yet is still able to discern wisely. He or she is also able to track details, and to see both the forest and the trees.

BE-ATTITUDE SELF ASSESSMENT

How developed is your core being for becoming a Legacy Leader in this Legacy Practice? After reading the descriptions of these BE-Attitudes above, rate yourself *(circle one)* on the following scale, then go on to the steps and questions that follow.

	BE-ATTITUDES of a Creator of Collaboration and Innovation	RATING: 5=all the time, 0=not at all
1	I am a trust builder.	5 4 3 2 1 0
2	I am an intuitive listener.	5 4 3 2 1 0
3	I am possibility-minded.	5 4 3 2 1 0
4	I am "charge-neutral."	5 4 3 2 1 0
5	I am mentally agile.	5 4 3 2 1 0

Where do your ratings fall? How many 5's? Any 2's or below? Any zeros? Here are some suggestions for building the core being of a Creator of Collaboration and Innovation.

1. ***Choose your two highest ratings***. Determine how you can leverage these strengths to be even more effective in developing and living your leadership legacy. ***Also choose two of your lowest*** rating attitudes to be your "work on" areas for improvement. Use the questions below to build your BE-attitudes.

2. ***Think of someone you know to be this***, to have this attitude, for each of the two areas you selected for improvement. For example, if you scored yourself low in being seamless in your behavior in all places, who do you know whose behavior *is* seamless (past or present)? Identify one person for each of the areas you want to develop and do the following exercises. Write the attitudes and person's name in the space provided:

	BE- ATTITUDE	Person I know who displays this be-attitude
1		
2		

Consider the following for each attitude, and person listed:

a. What does this person do that lets me, and others, know he or she is

   _____ (BE-Attitude)?

b. How can I emulate this behavior/attitude?

c. How will this behavior help me become a better leader? A Legacy Leader?

3. After completing the above steps, **make a commitment** to improve. Choose one of your "work on" attitudes each week, and focus on improving that attitude in all you think, do and speak.

   a. Be aware of your behavior and thought processes during the week, as they pertain to that attitude.
   b. Create a mental reminder that will alert you to old behavior and thought patterns you want to change.
   c. When you are alerted to old behavior and thought patterns, change them immediately, if possible. If not, use that experience to help remind you in the future. Consider what triggered this old behavior or attitude, and how you can respond differently in the future.
   d. Evaluate your week for progress and determine how you can improve this attitude next week.
   e. The following week, add another "work on" attitude as your focus, without neglecting the first one.
   f. Keep doing this until you notice a definite change (improvement), so that your improved attitude has become part of you, part of your core being as a Legacy Leader. Chances are if *you* notice an improvement, others will as well.
   g. If journaling is familiar and comfortable for you, consider keeping track of your BE-Attitude development. Brush away discouragement if things don't change immediately. They will, especially if this is the way you want to be. Sometimes we just need to rethink or reframe how we think and do.

WRITE ANY COMMENTS BELOW YOU THINK MIGHT HELP YOU STRENGTHEN THESE BE-ATTITUDES...

NOTES

DRILL DOWNS
Best Practice 2

The following section includes drill down *(more targeted and focused)* opportunities for each of the ten critical success skills for Best Practice 2. You may wish to complete the ones you have determined you need to strengthen first, but in order to truly round out your competencies and skills in this best practice, it is best to complete them all.

Drill Down 2:1

Best Practice 2:1

Creator of Collaboration and Innovation™

CRITICAL SUCCESS SKILL #1:
Personally create possibilities that are both innovative and sound for your organization.

Creating Possibilities...

Anyone can come up with an idea: **"Everyone who's ever taken a shower has an idea. It's the person who gets out of the shower, dries off and does something about it who makes a difference."** *(Nolan Bushnell, Founder of Atari)* This Critical Success Skill is about POSSIBILITIES, not just ideas. Possibilities take ideas to the next level, where they become innovative opportunities.

- Try completing the chart on the following page by listing 3 ideas YOU have had in the past 3 months to improve either your personal work responsibilities, or the functions within your area of responsibility. Now, briefly describe how you have taken these ideas and turned them into possibilities (opportunities). What was the result, or is the current status, of each? *(Make any additional comments here.)*

Something to Think About...

"Is it about creativity and speed? Or is it about cost cutting and risk avoidance? New ideas and opportunities? Or the stock market and layoffs? We all know the simple truth: You can't cost-cut your way to the future. The future depends on innovation."
A. Webber, et al. in "Fast Talk: The Innovation Conversation" Fast Company

Do you agree with the statement above? If so, how do you create possibilities for innovation within your organization, for yourself and for others?

★ ANSWERS

#	IDEA	CREATED POSSIBILITY	STATUS
1			
2			
3			

2:1
continued

TOP THREE

List your top 3 learnings, top 3 action plans, or top 3 personal reminders regarding this Critical Success Skill.

That are Both Innovative and Sound

Before ideas can become real possibilities and opportunities, they must first pass the feasibility and practicality tests.

- What questions do you ask in order to determine if ideas should become possibilities—if they are truly innovative and sound for your organization? (What criteria must be met?) List at least 5 questions/criteria to determine the innovation and soundness of any idea:

    1.

    2.

    3.

    4.

    5.

- Do you routinely screen ideas by these criteria? How, when, and what is the result?

Drill Down 2:2

Best Practice 2:2

CRITICAL SUCCESS SKILL #2:
Foster a learning, trusting environment where true collaboration and innovation are unleashed.

Creator of Collaboration and Innovation™

Foster a Learning, Trusting Environment

Sounds good, doesn't it? But how do you do it? Read this carefully:

"Businesses thrive when people trust one another. 'Social Capital' is the name that scholars have given to the trust relationships that make organizations work effectively..... [Leaders] need to make an intentional effort to build social capital in their organizations by...making connections, enabling trust, and fostering cooperation. 'Making connections' entails making a real commitment to retaining employees; promoting from within; giving people time and space to bond in person; facilitating personal conversations; and fostering durable networks both inside and outside the organization. 'Enabling trust' involves giving employees no reason to distrust (there are rules and the rules are followed, not bent for anyone's benefit); displaying trust toward employees, customers and suppliers; and sending clear signals that certain employee behaviors and outcomes are valued...'Fostering cooperation' entails giving people a common sense of purpose; rewarding cooperation; establishing rules for cooperation within the organization; and hiring team-oriented individuals rather than lone stars."

(from "How to Invest in Social Capital" by L. Prusack and D. Cohen in Harvard Business Review)

Something to Think About...

"We've found that we need to provide structure in order for innovation to occur...we started bringing these people together on a regular basis with some structure. Soon, ideas started to come out of the group. That's what we can do as leaders: Provide the forum and the structure to bring people together ...."
Rusty Rueff
Senior Vice President HR,
Electronic Arts, Inc.

Part of being a CREATOR of Collaboration and Innovation is CREATING the environment where this happens. What do you do to create an innovative environment within your organization?

ANSWERS

- Go back and underline all the major actions (above) that contribute to a learning and trusting environment. Are these things practiced in your organization, especially within your area of responsibility? What can be improved?

- What do YOU do personally, within your area of responsibility, to foster a learning, trusting environment BEYOND the things listed in the quotation above?

Unleashing Collaboration and Innovation

While all of the things above are excellent contributors to the presence of real collaboration and innovation, quite often YOU, as the leader, must encourage collaboration and innovation by making opportunities for both to be unleashed.

- How do you do this? (List at least 3 concrete ways you create opportunity for collaboration and encourage it on a day-to-day basis.)

- How do you encourage your team (as individuals and as a group) to be innovative?

2:2 continued

TOP THREE

List your top 3 learnings, top 3 action plans, or top 3 personal reminders regarding this Critical Success Skill.

Drill Down 2:3

Best Practice 2:3

Creator of Collaboration and Innovation™

CRITICAL SUCCESS SKILL #3:

Be a masterful listener for both what is said and what is not said.

Listening Masterfully

Being a good listener is a learned skill. Not everyone listens well, but everyone has the potential to listen well. It's a matter of discipline and the desire to hear others. That's where listening masterfully really begins—in the desire to understand and hear those around you. **"Being listened to and heard is one of the greatest desires of the human heart."** *(Richard Carlson)* This desire does not change in the business environment. Every human, no matter where he or she is encountered, desires to be heard. The real issue for the masterful listener is humility. Honestly listening, giving your whole attention (not just a token ear in passing) to another person means putting your own desires and your own needs aside, at least for that moment. It means you honestly desire to know and understand the other person, to really hear them.

- Are you a masterful listener? Describe your listening abilities.

Something to Think About...

"Effective leaders know how to listen empathetically ...thus legitimizing others' input. By doing so, they promote consensus building, and build strong teams. They coach others to do the same, and so create a culture of inclusiveness. They tend to be great listeners who capitalize on the ideas of others, and provide recognition for these ideas, yet they don't get bogged down in overly complicated dialogue. While they create learning organizations that place a high value on dialogue and continuous feedback, they know when to take action, when to 'fish or cut bait.'..."
Brian Ward, In "Lead People...Manage Things"

Are you an empathetic listener? Do you also know when to take action—when to "fish or cut bait?"

ANSWERS

- Do you "practice" listening well? Is this part of your leadership style? Describe.

- What advantages are there to you, and to your organization, when you listen masterfully?

- How does listening masterfully enhance collaboration?

2:3 continued

TOP THREE

List your top 3 learnings, top 3 action plans, or top 3 personal reminders regarding this Critical Success Skill.

Listening = Learning

What is SAID and what is NOT SAID

A masterful listener listens AND HEARS both what is spoken, and what is left unspoken. A good leader observes what is done, and what is undone. Quite often we learn more from what is not said, than from what the person actually speaks. Larry King is an expert at this. He once said **"I remind myself every morning: Nothing I say this day will teach me anything. So if I'm going to learn, I must do it by listening."** This is a profound statement. When we fill up the airwaves, we don't learn a thing, do we? And Mr. King only knows what questions to pose by listening mostly for what is UNSAID during his interviews. Do you do this? Are you an expert at hearing, or observing, what is not audible? Are you a DISCERNING listener?

Don't Listen	So-So Listener	Masterful Listener
0	5	10
• I don't care to listen • I don't need to listen • I already know what I need to know • I don't listen	• I listen when I have to, but don't make an effort beyond my need • Listening takes up too much time so I keep it to a minimum • When I do listen, I'm mostly thinking about my response, my needs • I don't usually learn too much by listening	• I desire to listen well, and honestly hear others • I need to listen to learn • I listen at every opportunity • I listen empathetically • I learn by also hearing what is NOT spoken • I am a discerning listener

Drill Down 2:4

Best Practice 2:4

CRITICAL SUCCESS SKILL #4:
Be comfortable not knowing "the answers" and learning from individual perspectives.

Creator of Collaboration and Innovation™

Comfort in the "Zone of Not Knowing"

"... leaders individually, or teams of leaders collectively, live in what we call the Zone of Not Knowing™. This zone is an unpredictable place ripe with opportunity, yet extremely uncomfortable for some who believe they need to know everything before they get out on the proverbial limb." (Smith and Sandstrom in "Accelerating Leader Learning in the Zone of Not Knowing")

Today's business world moves at the speed of light—quite literally—as knowledge is acquired and transactions are made through fiber optic cables that speed information from one side of the globe to the other in seconds. Every day, and sometimes every hour, the business landscape changes, both internally and externally. Leaders who thought they "knew it all" are finding quickly they know NOTHING at all at times. How do you keep up? By admitting you don't have all the answers, becoming a lifelong learner, and being open to the ideas and perspectives of others. John Wooden, the Hall of Fame basketball coach, said **"It's what you learn after you know it all that counts."**

Something to Think About...

"Learning, rather than planning, causes success, which very often comes from surprising sources which could not be planned for."
Brian Ward, In "The New Accountability"

On a scale of 1 to 5 *(5 being the highest)*, rate yourself in the following areas:

How comfortable are you not knowing "the answers?"	1	2	3	4	5
How open are you to learning from others?	1	2	3	4	5
How committed are you to being a learner?	1	2	3	4	5
How often do you SEEK the ideas and perspectives of others?	1	2	3	4	5
Do you listen masterfully to the perspectives of others? (Note: Critical Success Skill #3 for BP2 is vital here!)	1	2	3	4	5

Do you agree with this statement? Why or why not? What seemingly "surprising sources" at your organization could you learn from, and how?

ANSWERS

Comments: on your ratings

- What can you do to make all your responses to these questions a "5?" What is your action plan for this? Are you WILLING to do these things?

2:4
continued

TOP THREE

List your top 3 learnings, top 3 action plans, or top 3 personal reminders regarding this Critical Success Skill.

Collaborative Learning

So where do you get your answers? Some of them come obviously from research, from accessible information through conventional means. By and large, however, most of the leader's answers will come from human capital. Consider this: **"Human capital… carries a wealth of diverse information and knowledge. People now are more connected to global conversations and more interested in news around the world. Their expectations have changed from days past—they expect to be involved, to be valued, and utilized for their strengths. In essence, they want to contribute their brainpower and offer their wisdom. They are stakeholders with a vested interest in the success of the organization."**
(Smith and Sandstrom, above)

- Are you making full use of your human capital resources available to you within your organization? Describe. How can you improve, and how can you insure, a more collaborative learning environment in your area of responsibility, and throughout the organization?

Drill Down 2:5

Best Practice 2:5

Creator of Collaboration and Innovation™

CRITICAL SUCCESS SKILL #5:
Draw out differing perspectives and believe that disagreement is a learning opportunity.

Drawing out Differing Perspectives

"Leaders who make it a practice to draw out the thoughts and ideas of their subordinates and who are receptive even to bad news [or differing perspectives] will be properly informed." (L. B. Belker)

Today's leaders need every bit of information and every perspective they can effectively get their hands on. Differing perspectives are the fuel of healthy innovation and productive collaboration. The leader who does not welcome ideas, no matter if they agree or differ with his or hers, will cease to be a leader. It is the leader's responsibility to create the environment where these sometimes differing perspectives and ideas are freely offered and always valued. This environment of freedom of personal expression is built on the acceptance that every human being is unique and of value—and so are their opinions, perspectives and ideas. Winston Churchill said, **"No idea is so outlandish that it should not be considered with a searching, but at the same time a steady, eye."**

- Do you effectively draw out differing perspectives from your team members? How?

- What do you do with them?

Something to Think About...

"Unlike top management at Enron, exemplary leaders reward dissent. They encourage it. They understand that, whatever momentary discomfort they experience as a result of being told they might be wrong, it is more than offset by the fact that the information will help them make better decisions."
Warren Bennis
New York Times, 2/17/02

This is a strong statement. Do you agree? Rather than "dissent," perhaps "disagreement" better captures the concept behind this statement. Do you encourage and welcome disagreement? How, and why?

ANSWERS

Disagreement as a Path to Learning

Disagreement can lead to some of the best, most productive and **innovative collaboration**—if it is honored, respected and even encouraged. There can be many perspectives of the truth. Giving ear to each of these perspectives increases learning and provides a wider knowledge base for successful decision-making. Ovid said, **"You can learn from anyone, even your enemy."** There is always another perspective beyond your own. The wise leader learns to embrace moments of disagreement as pathways to deeper learning. More learning means more knowledge which means wiser choices. And what if, just maybe, you were "wrong?" Here's something to think about: **"The sufficiency of my merit is to know that my merit is not sufficient."** *(St. Augustine)*

- Recall a recent incident involving disagreement between you and your team members. How was it handled? What was the result? Did it lead to collaboration and innovation, or to some less desirable conclusion? What could you have done differently?

- How can YOU, as the leader in your area of responsibility, turn disagreement into powerful and innovative collaboration?

2:5 continued

TOP THREE

List your top 3 learnings, top 3 action plans, or top 3 personal reminders regarding this Critical Success Skill.

Drill Down 2:6

Best Practice 2:6

CRITICAL SUCCESS SKILL #6:
Keep in mind the bigger picture in order to ask timely, tough questions.

Creator of Collaboration and Innovation™

Something to Think About...

"The intellectual challenge of execution is in getting to the heart of an issue through persistent and constructive probing... Robust dialogue brings out reality, even when that reality makes people uncomfortable, because it has purpose and meaning. It is open, tough, focused, and informal. The aim is to invite multiple viewpoints, see the pros and cons of each one, and try honestly and candidly to construct new viewpoints...."
　　Bossidy & Charran in "Execution: The Discipline of Getting Things Done"

Do you "persistently and constructively probe" by asking tough and timely questions? How do you insure you get the right answers?

Keeping the Big Picture

So easy to say, not so easy to do. This basically involves Best Practice 1—Holding Vision and Values, but also implies knowing the "big things" while doing the "small things." Alvin Toffler said it quite succinctly: **"You've got to think about big things while you're doing small things, so that all the small things go in the right direction."** Overall strategic planning is one answer to this dilemma, but within the boundaries of the strategic plan will come the need for countless "Collaborative Conversations" to establish your direction and action at any given point along the path. This is why Best Practice 2, being a Creator of Collaboration and Innovation, is so important to being a Legacy Leader.

> *"The most serious mistakes are not being made as a result of wrong answers. The truly dangerous thing is asking the wrong questions."*
> — Peter Drucker

Asking Tough, Timely Questions

The successful leader cannot shy away from asking the questions that can yield the process for accomplishing vision and goals—even if those questions are tough to ask. CoachWorks has developed a model to not only ask the tough questions, but the right ones, as well as keeping the big picture in sight. The "Collaborative Conversation Model" can serve as a template to ensure that the questions will produce answers that lead to actions that take you and your organization where you want to be.

- ***Use this template to prepare relevant questions*** for a "Collaborative Conversation" with your team members.

Identify the problem, project or process you must move through (WHERE YOU ARE), then ask the hard questions that will provide the process to move you to WHERE YOU WANT TO BE. Design your questions to fit within each of these 5 process areas to bridge the gap. Review your questions. Do they

ANSWERS

cover all the needs, possibilities and desired outcomes? This template will help you ask the RIGHT questions in a timely manner while encouraging collaborative discussion, AND keeping the big picture in sight.

2:6 continued

TOP THREE

List your top 3 learnings, top 3 action plans, or top 3 personal reminders regarding this Critical Success Skill.

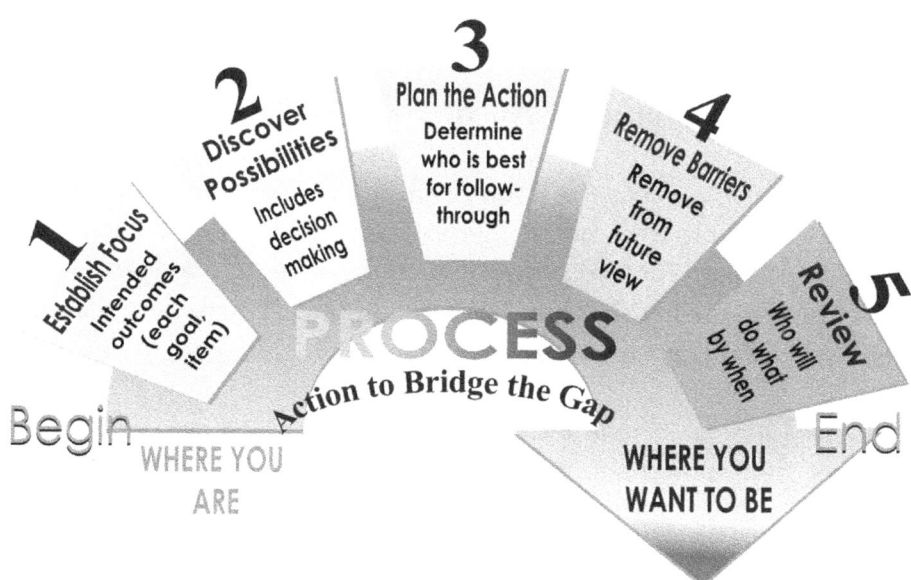

Collaborative Conversation Model™

- Design a specific *(one needed within your area)* Collaborative Conversation here:

Drill Down 2:7

Best Practice 2:7

CRITICAL SUCCESS SKILL #7:
Set the tone for thinking beyond where we are presently in order to innovate now for the future.

Creator of Collaboration and Innovation™

Something to Think About…

"It is change, continuing change, inevitable change, that is the dominant factor in society today. No sensible decision can be made any longer without taking into account not only the world as it is, but the world as it will be…This in turn, means that our statesmen, our businessmen, our everyman must take on a science fictional way of thinking."
Isaac Asimov

Hmmm. This is interesting. "Science fictional way of thinking?" What might be a better way to describe what Mr. Asimov is saying here, especially as it applies to today's business environment, and your organization in particular?

Setting the Tone for Thinking Beyond

Today's leader must see into the future, or at the very least BE AWARE of the future. It is too easy to become completely focused on yesterday and today, without proper regard for tomorrow. Success, however it is defined, should be an ever-elusive quality. Thomas J. Watson Jr. said, **"Whenever an individual or a business decides that success has been attained, progress stops."**

As the pace of change increases, the leader must keep one eye on the present and one eye on the future. It is the leader who holds the vision and sets the tone by bringing the future into the context of the present. The leader must see what might be invisible to others, and then translate it and give it form for his or her team members. The leader becomes the beacon, shining a light into the darkness of the future, drawing all eyes there. With enough light, people become accustomed to that darkness, and learn to move within it.

However, there is a balance to be achieved here. Too much thought and time spent in the future will deprive the present of its own attention. The leader is responsible for this balance in him or herself, as well as in others. Eric Hoffer addressed this balance: **"The leader has to be practical and a realist, yet must talk the language of the visionary and the idealist."**

★ ANSWERS

- How much time and thought do you regularly give to the future of your functional area, as well as the future of the organization?

2:7
continued

TOP THREE

List your top 3 learnings, top 3 action plans, or top 3 personal reminders regarding this Critical Success Skill.

- How do you translate this to your team members? Do you set the tone for their thinking, as well as your own?

- How do you maintain balance with the present and the future?

Innovating Now for the Future

Any organization that does not dream now about tomorrow, may never make it there. And in today's highly competitive business landscape, innovation is often the difference between organizational survival and extinction. Successful innovation does not happen fully in a vacuum—it requires collaboration and a boost of encouragement. Woodrow Wilson said, **"I not only use all the brains that I have, but all the brains I can borrow."**

- Do you regularly encourage your team members to be innovative and collaborative regarding the future? How do you do this? What is the result? How can you improve?

Drill Down 2:8

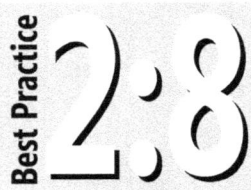

CRITICAL SUCCESS SKILL #8:
Project how ideas may play out in the organization and marketplace.

Creator of Collaboration and Innovation™

Something to Think About...

"Management is efficiency in climbing the ladder of success; leadership determines whether the ladder is leaning against the right wall."
Stephen R. Covey

No amount of innovation can insure the "ladder is leaning against the right wall." Whether you think this is part of your job responsibility or not, IT IS. Every leader should develop the art of successful projection of ideas. How does this relate to your organization, and in particular, your area of responsibility?

The Art of Projecting How Ideas Will "Play Out" in the Organization and the Marketplace

In an article titled *"7 Habits of Spectacularly Unsuccessful Executives"* (Fast Company), Sydney Finkelstein highlighted seven big mistakes *(made repeatedly, therefore habits!)* that executives have made which ensure failure of both their leadership and their organizations. The seventh "habit" is:

"#7 They stubbornly rely on what worked for them in the past."

Many CEOs on their way to becoming spectacularly unsuccessful accelerate their company's decline by reverting to what they regard as tried-and-true methods. In their desire to make the most of what they regard as their core strengths, they cling to a static business model. They insist on providing a product to a market that no longer exists, or they fail to consider innovations in areas other than those that made the company successful in the past. Instead of considering a range of options that fit new circumstances, they use their own careers as the only point of reference and do the things that made them successful in the past."

This bad habit is not limited to CEOs, and only deals with the mistake of relying upon what worked in the past to move into the future. This reveals a lack of innovation and forward thinking. In the last Drill Down, we discussed the need for innovating for the future. However, even if the leader *"sets the tone for thinking beyond where we are presently in order to innovate now for the future,"* success is not guaranteed. The **really critical factor** in planning for the future is the successful projection of how ideas will be received and

★ ANSWERS

"play out" in the organization and the marketplace. Without this, no amount of innovation, or reliance on tried and true tactics or strategy, will bring success. **This ability, an art in itself, coupled with innovation and collaboration, is what propels individuals and organizations into a successful future.**

- Have you tested your ability to successfully predict and project the success of ideas within the organization or marketplace? How do you do that, and what has been the result?

- How do you rate your ability as a "prognosticator?" (1 to 5, 5 being highest score) Explain.

- How can you improve your ability to project ideas successfully? (List at least 3 concrete steps you can take right now.)

    1.

    2.

    3.

- Do you consistently tie your projections to corporate vision and values?

2:8 continued

TOP THREE

List your top 3 learnings, top 3 action plans, or top 3 personal reminders regarding this Critical Success Skill.

Drill Down 2:9

Best Practice 2:9

CRITICAL SUCCESS SKILL #9:
Discern, and assist others to understand, when change needs to occur and when it does not.

Creator of Collaboration and Innovation™

Discerning the Need for Change

Increased innovation and collaboration have a natural side effect: increased change. Are you prepared for this? The need for change is inevitable, especially in this ever increasing pace of business and global changes. Jack Welch, former Chairman and CEO of GE Corporation said, **"If the rate of change on the outside exceeds the rate of change on the inside, the end is near."** Just as terminal, however, is change merely for the sake of change. The need for change cannot be determined on a whim, but on practical future thinking and concrete answers to the following questions:

1. Why doesn't the old way work any more? *(What is prompting this change?)*
2. What will this change provide for us?
3. Does this change support our vision and values, and overall strategy?
4. What's this change going to cost (dollars, people, time, etc.)?
5. Are the costs justified by the benefits of the proposed change?

Something to Think About...

- What has been your "track record" for discerning the need for change? Give examples and be specific.

"Effective change is not something you do to people. It's something you do with them."
— *Kenneth Blanchard and T. Waghorn*

- How can you improve this ability?

DISCERN: perceive, recognize, distinguish, discriminate

Change always involves others. Do you always consider how change will affect both outcomes and processes to achieve the outcomes? Do you consider how team members and others will be changed? Is change something you do WITH others?

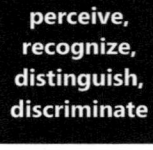
ANSWERS

Helping Others Understand the Need for Change

Mention the word "change" and people cringe. Change is inevitable, yet largely feared. The human creature naturally resists change. Even if for the better, change often brings discomfort to some. It becomes critical for the leader to be able to assist team members and others to understand when and why change needs to happen—and be just as alert to when it does NOT need to occur. Communication of vision, research, and background information and factors are the anchor of getting people onboard for such change. Consider this: **"Resistance to change is a survival mechanism. When someone suggests a new way of doing business to employees, they're offering a new, untested method of doing something. Employees have the right, even the responsibility to management and other stakeholders, to ask, "Why?" and to demand that the person proposing the change prove that what is being proposed is best for the company. Not protecting past successes and investments is irresponsible and a symptom of someone who doesn't care about the future."** (P. De Jager in "Resistance to Change: A New View of an Old Problem," The Futurist)

Does change need to occur? Do you KNOW it needs to occur? Do your team members know it? Consider this simple formula for change: **"The theory of tipping points 'hinges on the insight that in any organization, once the beliefs and energies of a critical mass of people are engaged, conversion to a new idea will spread like an epidemic, bringing about fundamental change very quickly.' A strong leader able to make calls for change, use resources wisely, motivate key people, and silence the opposition is needed."** (W. Chan Kim and Renee Mauborgne in "Tipping Point Leadership," Harvard Business Review.)

- How do you effectively communicate the need for change?

- What are the steps involved in the quote above? How can you make this a template for your future change implementations?

2:9 continued

TOP THREE

List your top 3 learnings, top 3 action plans, or top 3 personal reminders regarding this Critical Success Skill.

"The leader must know, must know that he knows, and must be able to make it abundantly clear to those around him that he knows."
Clarence Randall

Drill Down 2:10

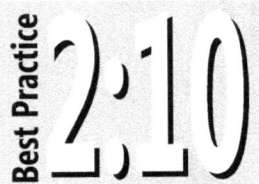
Best Practice 2:10

CRITICAL SUCCESS SKILL #10:
Be a masterful facilitator of conversations, allowing everyone to contribute their best thinking toward the task or issue at hand.

Creator of Collaboration and Innovation™

Being a Masterful Facilitator

This Best Practice is all about innovation and collaboration, and how you, as leader, can CREATE the environment where these flourish. In "The Right Stuff" Shari Caudron says an empowered leader **"knows how to facilitate the kind of group interaction that enables organization-wide success."** This kind of leader does not "hold court" in group or team discussions. He or she facilitates conversations by setting the tone and inviting high quality collaboration.

Tim Brown, President and CEO of Ideo Product Development, Inc., in an interview with other leaders about the power of innovation *(Fast Talk: The Innovation Conversation, Fast Company)* made the comment: **"Innovation is largely about making unexpected connections between things."** Mr. Brown was speaking about the search for new places to make connections between such things as product and market. However, there is another fundamental truth in his statement. The Legacy Leader will look for opportunities to create connections between PEOPLE, which in turn creates the opportunity for innovation and collaboration. These connections may be those found in the normal team meeting, or they may be those unexpected, arising from an openness to honestly hear everyone's best thinking—including the janitor or the employee in the mailroom. The leader who facilitates conversations makes the connections, plugs them in and lets them run. There are no circuit breakers or limit switches. The leader is merely the structural conduit for the electricity. Without artful facilitation, however, the electricity can run amok and overload the system.

Something to Think About...

"Only the leader can set the tone of the dialogue in the organization. Dialogue is the core of culture and the basic unit of work. How people talk to each other absolutely determines how well the organization will function."
Bossidy & Charran in "Execution: The Discipline of Getting Things Done"

Do you set the tone and masterfully facilitate conversations? What is the "tone of the culture" in your area of responsibility? Does everyone contribute his or her best? Why, or why not?

★ ANSWERS

- What is the difference between "holding court" and facilitating interaction in your team meetings? How do the results differ? *(Here's a hint: Robert A. Heinlein said, "**a committee [or a team] is a life form with six or more legs and no brain.**")*

- How do you set the tone, and what attitudes do you adopt and actions do you take as a facilitator in these meetings? Do you consider yourself a "masterful facilitator" of conversation?

Leading Others to Contribute Their Best Thinking

Facilitating conversations is only part of this equation. It isn't always difficult to get people talking, but getting them to share their best requires real leadership influence.

- What consistently motivates others to contribute their **best thinking**? List 5 elements that you believe result in the best of innovative and collaborative thinking—elements that YOU as leader must use as "facilitating" attitudes or actions. *Put them in play to test your thinking!*

    1.

    2.

    3.

    4.

    5.

- Now comes the hard part. How do you facilitate others to contribute their best thinking **AND remain focused on the task or issue at hand**? What has worked for you? What has not?

2:10 continued

TOP THREE

List your top 3 learnings, top 3 action plans, or top 3 personal reminders regarding this Critical Success Skill.

Building Trust That Leads to a Team's Collaborative Innovation Competencies

Legacy Leaders® establish environments that facilitate discovery of possibilities beyond conventional wisdom that taps the unique genius/gifts of all involved. The leader's job is to accept, honor, respect and facilitate each person's contributions/ideas, including options different than their own. Innovative possibilities result in leading-edge competitive positioning based on the vision and values template. This best practice fosters a "Star Wars" culture where Legacy Leaders® serve as Jedi Masters.

Successful teams must be committed to raise a standard in one area (team trust) in order to build competency in another area (creative collaboration). Review the Legacy Teams information at the right, score the index, and use the questions below to sharpen your skills.

THE TRUST INDEX
Circle the appropriate number that designates your comfort with building a "real" trust level in your team. Make sure that you are totally truthful with yourself.

SCORING PARAMETERS:
1—Not at all
2—Somewhat
3—Am able to do so
4—Do this easily
5—Insist on always doing this

#	Statement	1	2	3	4	5
1	As a team member/leader, I feel responsible for creating an environment of trust where members feel comfortable speaking their truth.	1	2	3	4	5
2	I own that my truth is merely my perception and never insist that my truth is the only truth.	1	2	3	4	5
3	I know that people may disagree with my perception of the truth and believe that when disagreements occur, so does learning.	1	2	3	4	5
4	I offer my thoughts, ideas, reservations, and concerns in order that collective wisdom may be enhanced.	1	2	3	4	5
5	I feel responsible for contributing as much to the collaboration of the team as possible.	1	2	3	4	5
6	I am not afraid to speak my truth to the team.	1	2	3	4	5
7	I neither embellish nor underreport my truth.	1	2	3	4	5
8	I do not withhold information that needs to be shared with the team.	1	2	3	4	5
9	I trust that team members will not "shoot the messenger."	1	2	3	4	5
10	I accept the information offered from other members as neither wrong nor right, but as added input.	1	2	3	4	5

SCORING: Add all circled numbers and find the category that fits you.
0 to 20   Your integrity isn't showing. Work with your Coach!
20 to 40 You have average trust levels.
40 to 50 Your team/employees/customers will appreciate your integrity

Legacy Teams:

Trust each other. This means they:
- Have high standards for their interactions and communications.
- Collaborate where options and outcomes are synergistic versus individualistic.
- Respectfully give and receive feedback to each other by speaking the truth.
- Support, learn from, and encourage each other with all ideas valued.

Imagine a meeting where:
- Members look forward to attending, come prepared, participate collaboratively.
- Members collectively approach each issue from "out-of-the-box" thinking.
- Real issues are drawn out and collaboratively managed.
- The environment is a learning environment.
- Differences are honored and respected.
- Communication is clear, laser and succinct.
- Disagreement is embraced and considered a time to learn additional information.
- Clarity is alive and well.
- Interaction is fun and invigorating.
- The work of the team is done in half the time with double the results.

Consider the following:

1. Describe the best collaborative/innovative team in which you have been a member. What guiding principles contributed to them being a committed and collaborative team?

2. In what ways will each of you take personal responsibility to contribute to the team trust and team collaboration? (How can you facilitate this?)

3. How will you hold yourself and each other accountable for team collaboration?

Developing the Art of Asking Leadership Questions

Leaders constantly model leadership competencies. One of the most important skills is the ability and courage to ask the tough and thought-provoking questions that create an environment for innovation within the team. There is an art to doing this. Challenge yourself to develop the art.

These questions can be used both in private conversations as well as team meetings. In the columns below, are suggestions to guide you in developing a repertoire of questions within the various areas of Legacy Leadership® competencies. As you practice, add more as you gain proficiency in this art.

Best Practice #1 Holder of Vision and Values™	Best Practice #2 Creator of Collaboration and Innovation™	Best Practice #3 Influencer of Inspiration and Leadership™	Best Practice #4 Advocator of Differences and Community™	Best Practice #5 Calibrator of Responsibility and Accountability™
• How does this forward our strategic vision? • How would that approach get us to our goal competitively? • What needs to happen so that we best serve the customer? • How does this ___ X ___ get us closer to where we want to be? • How does this fit with (match) what is being done in ___ X ___ (another business unit)? • What is our message? • Does this build shareholder value? • What questions will we be asking ourselves about this next year?	• How is this unique to anything you've done before? • What will we do to leverage what we've already been doing? • What is being done in other industries? Or not being done that could be? • Let's create something even beyond this. What hasn't been done before? • How can we construct the future so that this has a better outcome next time?	**Leader asks him/herself:** • How have I acknowledged each and every one? • How have I made each person feel extraordinary? • How have I let them know that I expect extraordinariness? • What strengths do they need to be recognized for? • How are we leveraging our successes? • How are you taking this message back to your people? *Add additional questions...*	• What resources can we draw upon to make this even better? • What strengths within this team are best suited for this project? • Who in the ranks needs to help us get this message out? • What do each of you want to contribute to this conversation? • What would it take to get going on this?	• What are the pros and cons of this approach? • What would keep us from being successful with this? • What outcomes do we want from this? • What are our successes? (What has worked and what could work better?) • Have we tied down the "what by when by whom?" • Who else needs to be involved with this?

Best Practice 2: Creator of Collaboration and Innovation™

Best Practice 2 Application Notes

Best Practice 2: Creator of Collaboration and Innovation™

Best Practice 2 Application Notes

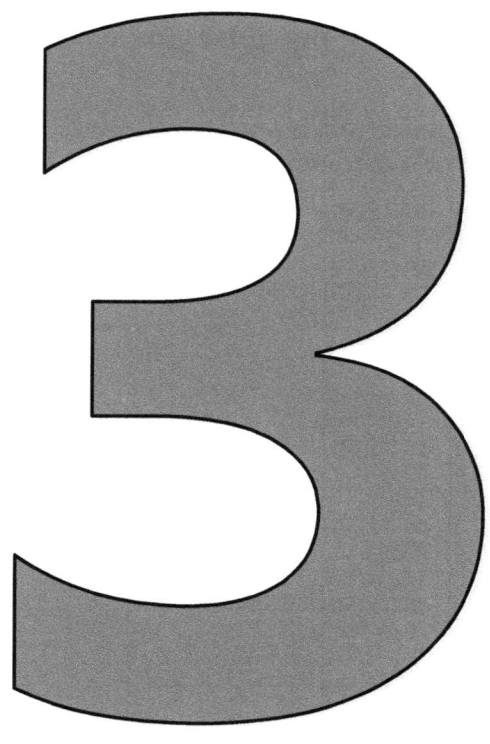

Best Practice 3
Influencer of Inspiration and Leadership™

WHERE ARE YOU NOW?

Take a current snapshot of your leadership skills and competencies for this Best Practice right now. A sample scoring sheet is shown below. The assessment for BP3 is found on the next page.

Instructions for Completion

For each Best Practice there is a set of ten descriptive statements. YOU ARE ASKED TO PROVIDE A RATING FOR **TWO QUESTIONS** FOR EACH STATEMENT (referred to as a "dual rating assessment"):

PERFORMANCE: How often **do I exhibit** this stated behavior/attitude?
EXPECTATIONS: How often is this stated behavior/attitude **expected to occur** in my position?

Read each statement carefully, and honestly rate yourself on a scale of 1 to 5 as follows:
- *This statement describes my actual current behavior/attitude (PERFORMANCE):*
- *The statement describes how often this behavior/attitude should occur (EXPECTATIONS):*
    1—Not At All
    2—Occasionally
    3—On Average
    4—Frequently
    5—Consistently

Rate yourself for BOTH Performance and Expectations using this scale.

After you have rated each statement, total each column under each of the two sets of responses (Performance and Expectations) and place the total score for each of the five columns in the blanks provided. Then add the column score total across from left to right for a total score for each set of ratings on each Best Practice. Graph your responses.

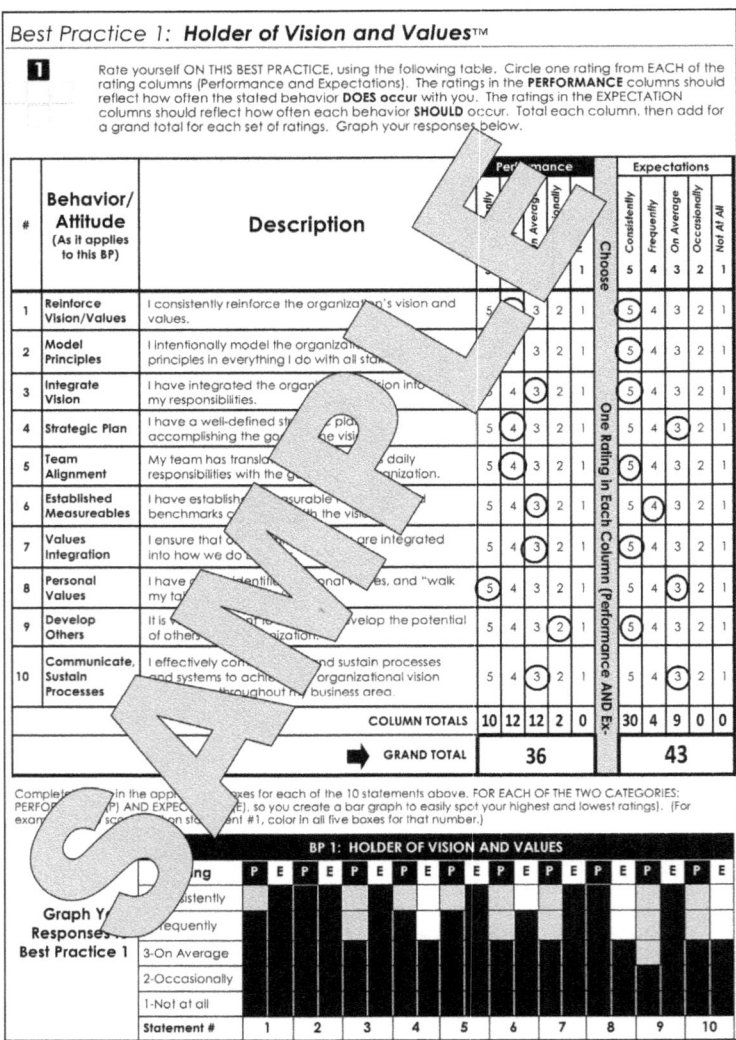

Legacy Leadership Application Workbook

Best Practice 3: **Influencer of Inspiration and Leadership**™

3

Rate yourself ON THIS BEST PRACTICE, using the following table. Circle one rating from EACH of the rating columns (Performance and Expectations). The ratings in the **PERFORMANCE** columns should reflect how often the stated behavior **DOES occur** with you. The ratings in the EXPECTATION columns should reflect how often each behavior **SHOULD** occur. Total each column, then add for a grand total for each set of ratings. Graph your responses below.

#	Behavior/Attitude (As it applies to this BP)	Description	Performance Consistently 5	Frequently 4	On Average 3	Occasionally 2	Not At All 1		Expectations Consistently 5	Frequently 4	On Average 3	Occasionally 2	Not At All 1
1	Develop Relationships	I am very adept at developing and maintaining relationships.	5	4	3	2	1	Choose One Rating in Each Column (Performance AND Expectations)	5	4	3	2	1
2	Energy to Influence	I use my emotional intelligence and positive energy to influence others.	5	4	3	2	1		5	4	3	2	1
3	Model Positive Perspective	I choose to model the positive perspective in all situations.	5	4	3	2	1		5	4	3	2	1
4	Evoke Best in Others	I bring out the best in people.	5	4	3	2	1		5	4	3	2	1
5	Acknowledge Contributions	I constantly acknowledge and recognize the attributes and contributions of others.	5	4	3	2	1		5	4	3	2	1
6	Delegate for Development	I intentionally delegate for the development of others.	5	4	3	2	1		5	4	3	2	1
7	Showcase Others	I lead with a constant focus on showcasing others rather than myself.	5	4	3	2	1		5	4	3	2	1
8	Inspiring Risk Taker	I have the ability and courage to take risks and inspire others to follow.	5	4	3	2	1		5	4	3	2	1
9	Minimize Negative	I am able to make tough decisions that have minimal negative impact.	5	4	3	2	1		5	4	3	2	1
10	Meet goals thru Others/Humility, Resolve	I lead with humility and fierce resolve to accomplish the goals of the organization through others.	5	4	3	2	1		5	4	3	2	1
		COLUMN TOTALS											
		➡ **GRAND TOTAL**											

Completely color in the appropriate boxes for each of the 10 statements above, FOR EACH OF THE TWO CATEGORIES: PERFORMANCE (P) AND EXPECTATION (E), so you create a bar graph to easily spot your highest and lowest ratings). (For example, if you scored "5" on statement #1, color in all five boxes for that number.)

Graph Your Responses to Best Practice 3

BP 3: INFLUENCER OF INSPIRATION AND LEADERSHIP™																					
Rating	P	E	P	E	P	E	P	E	P	E	P	E	P	E	P	E	P	E	P	E	
5-Consistently																					
4-Frequently																					
3-On Average																					
2-Occasionally																					
1-Not at all																					
Statement #	1		2		3		4		5		6		7		8		9		10		

APPLY THE BASICS

Critical Success Skills: Core Competencies

Legacy Leaders are trail blazers, forging the path to great leadership with positive influence so that everyone is lifted up to be the best he or she can be. People are invited, not commanded, to contribute from their strengths and are filled with energy to deliver high quality outcomes. This leader is self-inspired, and knows what inspires others. Influencing *inspiration* requires including the heart in all processes, connecting personally with others, and valuing them individually and corporately. To successfully influence *leadership*, the leader makes a conscious choice to be a positive presence that instills confidence rather than destroying it, and actively seeks ways to uplift and enhance the leadership growth of others. The ten critical success skills that compose this best practice include certain behaviors that take inspiration and leadership from mere words on a page to active influencers for shaping corporate success, and tomorrow's leaders, and exchanges organizational command-and-control for a nurturing structure and environment.

1. Be very adept at developing and maintaining relationships.
2. Use emotional intelligence and positive energy to influence others.
3. Choose to model the positive perspective in all situations.
4. Bring out the best in people.
5. Constantly acknowledge and recognize the attributes and contributions of others.
6. Intentionally delegate for the development of others.
7. Lead with a constant focus on showcasing others, not self.
8. Have the ability and courage to take risks and inspire others to follow.
9. Be able to make tough decisions with minimal negative impact.
10. Lead with humility and unwavering resolve to accomplish the goals of the organization through others.

Essence: *Being* a Legacy Leader
BE-Attitudes of an Influencer of Inspiration and Leadership

Among the long list of qualities and attitudes of a great leader in this Legacy Practice we would expect to find such things as humble, inspirational, others-centered, passionate, and an opportunity seeker (for others), to name just a few. However, we have already stated that Legacy Leaders have a solid platform of attitudes that set them apart from all other leaders. This leader intentionally influences others through a set of both natural and highly refined basic attitudes that we have delineated for this Legacy Practice. These attitudes mark the very core identity of Legacy Leaders. We have listed the features we consider the Top Five BE-attitudes for your consideration in this Legacy Practice. These are not listed in any order of importance. Brief descriptions follow. *A Legacy Leader, an Influencer of Inspiration and Leadership, IS:*

> ☐ **Relationship-Driven**
> ☐ **Impact Aware**
> ☐ **Self-Inspired**
> ☐ **A Mentor**
> ☐ **Positive**

1. **Relationship-Driven**
This person is not just relational, but relationship-driven. This person realizes that everything in life, including business, is driven by relationships and he or she is therefore driven to build and maintain relationships. These people don't just "get along" with people, they must connect with them to thrive.

2. **Impact-Aware**
This person has developed a discernment that allows them to be consciously aware of surroundings, including his or her own impact on situations and other people. These people understand the value and the responsibility of their impact on other people, and as such are intentional about their influence. They know well the concepts of cause and effect, actions and reactions, and behavior and consequences.

3. **Self-Inspired**
This person does not need others to inspire self. These people are able to draw personal inspiration from a variety of sources. In this regard they are not externally driven, but self-driven. They are fully aware of what inspires them and are able to seek that inspiration on their own. They are authentic, confident and aware of personal values.

4. **A Mentor**
This person may or may not have an official role or title as mentor, but they have an inborn attitude of coming alongside others in order to build them and encourage them (mentor-minded). He or she constantly seeks ways to improve others, to develop them, advance them and showcase them. These people have a self-awareness that their own development and experiences may be of benefit to others, and desire to share learning to move others forward.

5. **Positive**
This person thinks and behaves in positive ways. He or she has an underlying positive viewpoint, and is always searching for (mindful of) the positive avenues and attitudes in any situation. This attitude does not mean this person is not realistic. They are able to think realistically, yet with a positive end point (outcome) in mind.

BE-ATTITUDE SELF ASSESSMENT

How developed is your core being for becoming a Legacy Leader in this Legacy Practice? After reading the descriptions of these BE-Attitudes above, rate yourself *(circle one)* on the following scale, then go on to the steps and questions that follow.

	BE-ATTITUDES of an Influencer of Inspiration and Leadership	RATING: 5=all the time, 0=not at all
1	I am relationship-driven.	5 4 3 2 1 0
2	I am impact aware.	5 4 3 2 1 0
3	I am self-inspired.	5 4 3 2 1 0
4	I am a mentor.	5 4 3 2 1 0
5	I am positive.	5 4 3 2 1 0

Where do your ratings fall? How many 5's? Any 2's or below? Any zeros? Here are some suggestions for building the core being of an Influencer of Inspiration and Leadership.

1. **Choose your two highest ratings.** Determine how you can leverage these strengths to be even more effective in developing and living your leadership legacy. **Also choose two of your lowest** rating attitudes to be your "work on" areas for improvement. Use the questions below to build your BE-attitudes.

2. **Think of someone you know to be this**, to have this attitude, for each of the two areas you selected for improvement. For example, if you scored yourself low in being seamless in your behavior in all places, who do you know whose behavior *is* seamless (past or present)? Identify one person for each of the areas you want to develop and do the following exercises. Write the attitudes and person's name here:

    ATTITUDE   PERSON I KNOW WHO DISPLAYS THIS ATTITUDE
    1.
    2.

    Consider the following for each attitude, and person listed:

    a. What does this person do that lets me, and others, know he or she is

       _____ (BE-Attitude)?

b. How can I emulate this behavior/attitude?

c. How will this behavior help me become a better leader? A Legacy Leader?

3. After completing the above steps, ***make a commitment*** to improve. Choose one of your "work on" attitudes each week, and focus on improving that attitude in all you think, do and speak. Practice these things for each BP you work on:

   a. Be aware of your behavior and thought processes during the week as they pertain to that attitude.

   b. Create a mental reminder that will alert you to old behavior and thought patterns you want to change.

   c. When you are alerted to old behavior and thought patterns, change them immediately, if possible. If not, use that experience to help remind you in the future. Consider what triggered this old behavior or attitude, and how you can respond differently in the future.

   d. Evaluate your week for progress and determine how you can improve this attitude next week.

   e. The following week, add another "work on" attitude as your focus, without neglecting the first one.

   f. Keep doing this until you notice a definite change (improvement), so that your improved attitude has become part of you, part of your core being as a Legacy Leader. Chances are if *you* notice an improvement, others will as well.

   g. If journaling is familiar and comfortable for you, consider keeping track of your BE-Attitude development. Brush away discouragement if things don't change immediately. They will, especially if this is the way you want to be. Sometimes we just need to rethink or reframe how we think and do.

WRITE ANY COMMENTS BELOW YOU THINK MIGHT HELP YOU STRENGTHEN THESE BE-ATTITUDES...

NOTES

DRILL DOWNS
Best Practice 3

The following section includes drill down *(more targeted and focused)* opportunities for each of the ten critical success skills for Best Practice 3. You may wish to complete the ones you have determined you need to strengthen first, but in order to truly round out your competencies and skills in this best practice, it is best to complete them all.

Drill Down 3:1

CRITICAL SUCCESS SKILL #1:

Be very adept at developing and maintaining relationships.

Influencer of Inspiration and Leadership™

Developing and Maintaining Relationships

Best Practice 3 is the heart of Legacy Leadership®, and this Critical Success Skill is the heart of this Best Practice. The distinguishing mark of a great leader is the importance they place on personal relationships. Obviously, a certain level of relationship is necessary in order to function properly in business. However, the Legacy Leader® goes beyond the minimum standards for relationships to the realm of genuine caring and real knowledge about team members.

Something to Think About...

- Think about each of your team members individually. Can you say, honestly, that you care about them and both their personal and organizational success? If so, how do you show it? Are there any in particular with whom you need to work to further develop a caring (and working) relationship? What can you do about those?

"Eventually relationships determine the size and length of leadership."
John C. Maxwell

"In organizations, real power and energy is generated through relationships. The patterns of relationships and the capacities to form them are more important than tasks, functions, roles, and positions."
Margaret Wheatly

- Can you say that you "understand" your team members as individuals; that is, do you KNOW them, know their abilities, know their challenges and show your understanding? Consider this: **"Nothing is more validating and affirming than feeling understood. And the moment a person begins feeling understood is when that person becomes far more open to influence**

Think about these statements. Do you agree? Why or why not? Have you built solid relationships with your team members? With others inside and outside the organization?

ANSWERS

and change." *(Steven Covey)* How does understanding your team members help you become more of an INFLUENCER?

3:1
continued

TOP THREE

List your top 3 learnings, top 3 action plans, or top 3 personal reminders regarding this Critical Success Skill.

- Legacy Leaders® desire the success of those around them—those they lead. They actively seek to build more leaders. Can you say that? How do you demonstrate that?

- Caring about individuals is only one part of developing and maintaining relationships. According to Brian Ward in "The New Accountability," the **OLD accountability has a focus on the individual, while the NEW accountability sees the individual as part of a "vibrant collaborative network."** With this in mind, how do you INFLUENCE the development of relationships among your team members?

Drill Down 3:2

Best Practice 3:2

CRITICAL SUCCESS SKILL #2:

Use emotional intelligence and positive energy to influence others.

Influencer of Inspiration and Leadership™

Something to Think About...

"The leader's mood and behaviors drive the moods and behaviors of everyone else. Therefore, a leader's premier—even primal—task is emotional leadership...Brain research shows we have open-loop limbic systems that allow people to affect each other's physiologies and emotions. Emotions spread irresistibly, and moods that start at the top tend to move the fastest—because everyone watches the boss."
  D. Goleman; R. Boyatzis, A. McKee in "Primal Leadership" Harvard Business Review

What do you think about these statements? Are they true, in your experience? If so, what is your responsibility as a leader?

Emotional Intelligence

Emotional Intelligence is a hot topic in the business world. It is a term that has been used for some time now to relate to a person's both innate and developed abilities in the areas of self-awareness (particularly as it applies to personal emotions), self-confidence, self-control, self-motivation and people skills such as empathy, understanding others, influence, conflict management, etc. There is a wealth of information readily available on Emotional Intelligence; particularly well-known is Daniel Goleman's first book on the topic in 1995. Some research has suggested that Emotional Intelligence can account for up to 85% of the success (or failure) of leaders today.

- We are assuming that you are well aware of the concept of Emotional Intelligence, and even beyond that, are aware of your own. This Drill Down does not seek to assess your EI, but to make you aware of its use as an INFLUENCER within leadership. Considering what you know about your personal EI, how does this affect (either positively or negatively) your ability to influence others? (If you need some guidance in answering this, consider the areas listed above—self-confidence, self-awareness, etc.)

ANSWERS

- Research has also suggested that EI can be developed. Even though we are probably born with certain EI tendencies, we can work to change and improve the ones that impact us and others negatively. What areas of your EI need work? How can you improve them?

3:2 continued

TOP THREE

List your top 3 learnings, top 3 action plans, or top 3 personal reminders regarding this Critical Success Skill.

Positive Energy

This term is linked strongly with EI, but it is also a more comprehensive term that relates to your overall attitude of leadership. One definition we found is that positive energy in leadership is the operation from hope of success rather than fear of failure.

- Does your work reflect positive energy? How? If not, why not? How would you define positive energy in leadership?

Drill Down 3:3

CRITICAL SUCCESS SKILL #3:

Choose to model the positive perspective in all situations.

Influencer of Inspiration and Leadership™

Making a Choice

Leadership is all about choices, and our attitude of leadership and foundational perspective is one of the biggest choices of all. We CHOOSE whether we model the negative, or the positive, in all situations. This does not mean that you avoid being realistic. Being positive means that you are truthful and that your message is delivered in a way that can be respectfully given and heard.

- A Legacy Leader chooses to model the positive perspective at all times. Does this describe you—do you make this conscious choice? Why or why not?

- Rose Fass, Principal and Partner with the Center for Transformation at Xerox said, **"In becoming a more effective leader, you have to practice the practice of leadership."** What does this have to do with modeling a positive perspective?

Something to Think About...

"Our personal power and potential for well-being are shaped by the negative or positive ways we think."
—Herbert Benson

What does "person power" mean to you, especially as an INFLUENCER in your organization? How does the way you think, positively or negatively, shape your potential for well-being, personally, professionally and organizationally?

ANSWERS

- Describe a specific time when the situation seemed negative, but you were able to approach it with a positive perspective, yielding positive results.

Positive Perspective

When viewed from an emotional standpoint, the word "negative" tends to leave us cold and dark—repelled. In contrast, the word "positive" connotes warmth and light—attraction. Consider this: **"...'warmth' emerged as a consistent and robust predictor of leadership effectiveness...this factor was consistently correlated with [other leadership skills]. People high on warmth are described as easygoing, adaptable, warm-hearted, attentive to people, frank, expressive, trustful, co-operating and participating."** *(Note: This article continues to indicate that warmth is a necessary but not sufficient [alone] condition for leadership.) (From "A Psychological Analysis of Leadership Effectiveness" by L. Hartman in Strategy and Leadership)*

- Are you a leader with "warmth?" Do you connect easily with others? How so? Do others see you this way? If not, what can you do about it?

- How does viewing things with a positive perspective affect your "warmth" rating as a leader?

3:3 continued

TOP THREE

List your top 3 learnings, top 3 action plans, or top 3 personal reminders regarding this Critical Success Skill.

Drill Down 3:4

Best Practice 3:4

Influencer of Inspiration and Leadership™

CRITICAL SUCCESS SKILL #4:
Bring out the best in people.

Bringing out the Best

This is a seemingly simple statement that defies description. Just exactly HOW do we bring out the best in others? How has the best been brought out in you? Doing this is not easily elaborated and varies from leader to leader, and team member to team member. There are some commonalities, however, and one of those is to always ENCOURAGE and EXPECT the best. How do you do it? Let's get practical.

- List 5 ways you can, in general, bring out the best in people you work with:

  1.

  2.

  3.

  4.

  5.

Something to Think About...

"The reward for work is not what you get for it, but what you become from it."
—H. Rubin in Fast Company "The Perfect Vision of Dr. V" quoting Dr. Govindappa Venkataswamy

We know not everyone will agree with this. Do you? If so, how would you convince your team members that this is true? What does this have to do with bringing out the best in others?

★ ANSWERS

- Now get specific. List 3 of your team members. Next to each name, give 3 SPECIFIC ways you can bring out the best in each of them—as individuals. Then, do it!

Name	3 Specific Ways to Bring Out the Best in This Person

3:4 continued

TOP THREE

List your top 3 learnings, top 3 action plans, or top 3 personal reminders regarding this Critical Success Skill.

Influencing Inspiration to Communicate the Best

While bringing out the best in people is undeniably a difficult to define subject, it most definitely includes inspiring communication. This Best Practice is all about INFLUENCING, and bringing out the best in people includes inspiring them to do and be their best. One of the most rewarding ways to do this is through the **artistry and skill of storytelling**. Research reveals today that storytelling in business is one of the most powerful (and inspiring) communication tools. Consider this: **"While management philosophies come and go and new approaches to running 21st century businesses and institutions are introduced, one thing may be immutable—the need to share stories that inspire, teach, and guide the organization."** *(International Storytelling Center)* And this: **"A good story efficiently and powerfully conveys knowledge that often cannot be communicated as effectively in other ways. Stories are powerful because they show us rather than tell us, dramatically enacting a truth that can move us and influence the way we see things."** *(Stephen Denning, Director of World Bank's Knowledge Management Program).*

- Do you know how to use stories to inspire and influence others to be their best, to communicate in ways that inspire and motivate? If so, give an example of a story (briefly) from your business repertoire, and one about yourself. If not, what can you, and will you, do about it? Are you willing to learn this skill? Are you willing to share both your successes and your mistakes?

Drill Down 3:5

Best Practice 3:5

CRITICAL SUCCESS SKILL #5:
Constantly acknowledge and recognize the attributes and contributions of others.

Influencer of Inspiration and Leadership™

Acknowledge and Recognize

One of the foundations of Legacy Leadership is that it is **OTHER-centered**, instead of self-centered. The focus of a Legacy Leader is on building up others. To really understand this Critical Success Skill, it should be noted that each of these words, *acknowledge* and *recognize*, can have two different meanings here:

Acknowledge: to admit to be real or true; AND to show or express appreciation or gratitude for something or someone

Recognize: to identify or become aware of; AND to formally reward

Putting it together, there is a sequence of events that must occur to completely satisfy this CSS:

1. Identify or become aware of the attributes and contributions of others
2. Admit that they are real and true, worthwhile and praiseworthy
3. Show or express appreciation for them in specific terms
4. Formally reward them

- Are you aware of, and have you identified the attributes and contributions of your team members? Are you OTHER-centered enough to be looking for them, to know your team members well enough to know them?

Something to Think About...

"If you wish others to believe in you, you must first convince them that you believe in them."
—Harvey Mackay

This is a foundational truth in human relationships. What does this have to do with being an INFLUENCER of Inspiration and Leadership? How do you convince your team members that you believe in them?

ANSWERS

- Can you admit they are real and true, and worthy of commendation? (In other words, are you not so lost in self that you can acknowledge the contributions of others?)

- Do you express appreciation for these attributes and contributions of others? How?

- Do you formally reward them? How? What is an appropriate reward or acknowledgement and recognition of attributes and contributions among your team members?

- Give a specific example of a recent acknowledgement/recognition you gave to one of your team members for his or her attributes/contributions.

- Here's a difficult question. Is your heart in this, or is it just for show? (Be honest!)

- John Ashcroft, former Chairman of Coloroll, said **"The worst mistake a boss can make is not to say 'well done.'"** Do you agree? Why or why not?

3:5 continued

TOP THREE

List your top 3 learnings, top 3 action plans, or top 3 personal reminders regarding this Critical Success Skill.

Drill Down 3:6

Best Practice 3:6

CRITICAL SUCCESS SKILL #6:

Intentionally delegate for the development of others.

Influencer of Inspiration and Leadership™

Something to Think About...

"The ultimate test for a leader is not whether he or she makes smart decisions and takes decisive action, but whether he or she teaches others to be leaders and builds an organization that can sustain its success even when he or she is not around."
—Noel Tichy

This is the bottom line of this Best Practice— Influencing Leadership and inspiring the growth of others. Is your goal to merely "do the job" or is it to sustain the success of your organization by purposely building other leaders? How do you do this?

Delegating for Development

We all know that a good leader must be a good delegator. The intentional delegation that marks a Legacy Leader®, however, is thoughtful and deliberate with the specific intent to develop others. Assigning tasks is one thing; developing others through delegation is the hallmark of Legacy Leadership®. This is what **LEGACY** in leadership is all about. Leaders may randomly distribute tasks in order to "get the job done." While this is important, a Legacy Leader® knows the attributes and skills of team members and what will challenge them to growth and future success— delegation becomes a pathway to development.

Delegation also has its obvious rewards for the leader as well. Consider this: **"The more you share, the easier your job becomes. People want challenge and will gladly take a project from you. Then, you can really exercise your expertise by providing advice and creative ideas, without getting buried in the unchallenging details. The more information you share, the less your employees need close management, since they will understand where to take action to solve problems. Once employees are experienced enough to make their own decisions, they become more enthusiastic and motivated."** *(From "Lessons to Be Learned From Bad Bosses" by Joan Lloyd www.JoanLloyd.com)* This quote is from a section describing the "Hoarder," the leader who "squirrels away information, power and/or satisfying work." What you may find "unchallenging" (according to this quote), another may experience as the very road to growth.

ANSWERS

- Are you a delegator? Describe your delegation skills. Do you delegate for the right reasons? Do you delegate merely to "get the job done," or do you deliberately delegate for the development of others? Give some thought to this and describe briefly how you can use delegation as a development tool for the advancement of others.

3:6 continued

TOP THREE

List your top 3 learnings, top 3 action plans, or top 3 personal reminders regarding this Critical Success Skill.

We think Mr. Tichy has captured the essence of Legacy Leadership®. Consider this: **"Why do some companies succeed while others fail? As an organizational psychologist and management consultant for nearly 30 years, the answer I have come up with is that winning companies win because they have good leaders who nurture the development of other leaders at all levels of the organization."** *(from "Winning Companies Build Leaders At Every Level, by Noel M. Tichy)*

- Do you agree? Why or why not? In this regard, are YOU a Legacy Leader? Describe.

Drill Down 3:7

CRITICAL SUCCESS SKILL #7:

Lead with a constant focus on showcasing others rather than self.

Influencer of Inspiration and Leadership™

Showcasing Others

As we read the current headlines of scandals within the sacred halls of leadership in the corporate world, one common denominator among those responsible for such a blight on business today is easy to spot—selfishness. The focus and motivation of all their activities is SELF. Consider this: **"An authentic leader acts in ways which serve to elevate those around him."** *(Sean M. Georges)* It is, unfortunately, human nature to desire to elevate SELF, rather than others. Therefore, it is a conscious choice and a firm commitment that must be made to do what is contrary to human tendency—to showcase others. This Focus goes hand-in-hand with the previous one which discusses the development of others. Part of developing and building others is showcasing them, putting them in the spotlight, elevating them, and seeking their success—often before our own. Is this possible?

- Can you honestly (!) say that you lead with a constant focus on showcasing others rather than self? Do you desire to "elevate" those around you? Have you made a choice and commitment to do this with your team members? Describe your plan and actions to showcase others. Anything missing? Quite often this is a matter of the heart, rather than the head. If you don't honestly desire to do this, it will be a very difficult task, constantly battling self. Are you ABLE to do this? How and why?

Something to Think About...

"Set the course of your life by the three stars—sincerity, courage and unselfishness. From these flow a host of other virtues...He who follows them will obtain the highest type of success, that which lies in the esteem of others."
—Monroe E. Deutsch

Do you agree with this statement? How are each of these qualities—sincerity, courage and unselfishness—demonstrated in showcasing others? How do you do this in your organization?

One man has even gone so far as to equate being successful or unsuccessful

 ANSWERS

in this way: **"Successful people are always looking for opportunities to help others. Unsuccessful people are always asking, 'What's in it for me?'"** *(Brian Tracy)* Robert Hargrove said, **"True leaders are not selfish. They share successes and their power."** This seems SO contrary to what we experience in corporate communities today. Is it in yours?

- How does success (whether personal, professional, or organizational) relate to your ability to showcase others? Make a personal/professional connection with this and describe.

- In the interest of developing your ability to become an inspiring storyteller, can you think of a brief but powerful story, whether within your experience or outside, to illustrate these concepts quickly and dramatically?

3:7 continued

TOP THREE

List your top 3 learnings, top 3 action plans, or top 3 personal reminders regarding this Critical Success Skill.

We couldn't resist this...

"Mr. Big Shot makes a big target. Eventually, his arrogance will catch up with him. His employees will resent his puffery and they will not protect his back. When he is about to step on a political landmine, they will merely smile. As soon as you start thinking you are better than the 'little people' in your department or your company, you've forgotten the lesson that you are there to serve them, not the other way around."

*Joan Lloyd
from "Lessons to Be Learned From Bad Bosses"
www.JoanLloyd.com*

Drill Down 3:8

Best Practice 3:8

CRITICAL SUCCESS SKILL #8:
Have ability and courage to take risks and inspire others to follow.

Influencer of Inspiration and Leadership™

Something to Think About...

"Good leaders make people feel that they're at the very heart of things, not at the periphery. Everyone feels that he or she makes a difference to the success of the organization. When that happens people feel centered and that gives their work meaning."
—Warren G. Bennis and Burt Nanus

How does this statement apply to your ability and courage to take risks and inspire others to follow? Are your team members "at the very heart" of your risk taking? How? What are the corporate results?

Taking Risks that Inspire Others to Follow

This success skill is not a treatise on the "how-to's" or benefits of risk taking. Rather, it is about how a Legacy Leader models this ability courageously IN ORDER to inspire others to follow. Obviously, feasibility, practicality and plain old common sense must be factors in risk taking. We're talking about informed and intelligent risks. **"To be sure, reckless actions that risk too much in circumstances that are totally unfamiliar are foolhardy."** *(Paul Willax in "Informed Risk-Taking is Better Than Playing it Safe," Business First)* The kind of risk taking Mr. Willax refers to here will never inspire anyone to follow—quite the opposite.

What this Critical Success Skill refers to is more accurately summarized in this statement: **"People will rise to meet seemingly insurmountable obstacles and challenges if they understand the worthiness of the personal sacrifices and effort. Supporting that understanding must be mentors who provide leadership; without both ingredients, a cause will go unrealized and a mission is likely to fail."** *(Glenn R. Jones, "Creating a Leadership Organization with a Learning Mission" in The Organization of the Future.)* The Legacy Leader makes deliberate and well-thought out choices, not only for the advancement of the organization, but as a mentor who shows the way, inspiring others to have courageous expectations of making a **"dent in the universe"** *(as Steve Jobs has said).*

★ ANSWERS

- Take a look again at the quote by Glenn Jones. Evaluate the components he states are required for successful "missions." List them here. What other qualities do you think are necessary? How do these relate to having the "ability and courage to take risks and inspire others to follow?"

- What kind of risk taker are you, especially as it applies to your area of responsibility? Describe your ability and courage on a scale of 1 to 10, with 1 being "milquetoast" and 10 being "ready to leap in the moment." Describe how you approach risk taking, and why you gave yourself this rating.

- Developing risk-taking skills is one thing. Inspiring others to follow is another. How can you take risks AND inspire others? What does this look like? Do you DO it? What advantage does this behavior have to you, your team members, and your organization?

- Leadership courage is also the ability to speak up at all times even when the message is a difficult one to deliver. Do you do this consistently, WITH a positive perspective? How?

3:8 continued

TOP THREE

List your top 3 learnings, top 3 action plans, or top 3 personal reminders regarding this Critical Success Skill.

Drill Down 3:9

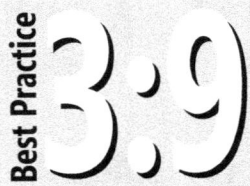

Best Practice 3:9

CRITICAL SUCCESS SKILL #9:
Be able to make tough decisions that have minimal negative impact.

Influencer of Inspiration and Leadership™

Something to Think About...

"...individuals were then asked what helped them most in their quest to become a good leader. Nine out of ten said they had a role model; either a positive one whom they learned to emulate, or a negative one whose style they learned to avoid."

—Shari Caudron
"The Right Stuff"

What kind of impact do your decisions have? When you make a tough choice, would you say your co-workers might emulate your style, or avoid it? How do you handle the fallout from your decisions? With emphasis on the positive or the negative?

Tough Decisions—Minimal Negatives

Tough decisions often mean some negative impact. This Critical Success Skill is about minimizing the negatives and emphasizing the positives, especially as they affect your team members and the organization as a whole. Situations requiring tough decisions may indicate adversity or obstacles, which can seem to overpower the potential positives. How can you, a role model for everyone in your organization—not just your immediate team members—use decision making, especially the tough choices, to model behavior that enhances learning and opens doors to opportunity for future success?

Consider the following statements, then provide your comments on how each one relates to your behavior as a Legacy Leader®, able to make tough decisions that have minimal negative impact—and can, in fact, lead to possibility. Remember, the focus here is not so much on MAKING the decisions, but on insuring positive, not negative, attitudes and impacts.

- *"Problems are only opportunities in work clothes."* - Henri Kaiser

- What makes an extraordinary leader? **"The ability to conquer adversity and emerge stronger and more committed than ever....The essentials of leadership include: the ability to engage others in shared meaning; a distinctive and compelling voice; and a sense of integrity. But the most important skill is 'adaptive capacity' or the ability to overcome adversity and come out stronger. The hardiness and ability to grasp context that make up adaptive capacity allow people to not only survive, but to learn from an ordeal."** - *Warren G. Bennis and Robert J. Thomas, "The Crucibles of Leadership," in Harvard Business Review*

- **"Success is going from failure to failure without a loss of enthusiasm."** - *Winston Churchill*

- **"The majority see the obstacles; the few see the objectives; history records the successes of the latter, while oblivion is the reward of the former."** - *Alfred Armand Montapert*

- We couldn't resist this one! **"Is your cucumber bitter? Throw it away. Are there briars in your path? Turn aside. That is enough. Do not go on and say, 'Why were things of this sort ever brought into the world?'"** - *Marcus Aurelius*

3:9 continued

TOP THREE

List your top 3 learnings, top 3 action plans, or top 3 personal reminders regarding this Critical Success Skill.

Drill Down 3:10

CRITICAL SUCCESS SKILL #10:
Lead with humility and unwavering resolve to accomplish the goals of the organization through others.

Influencer of Inspiration and Leadership™

Something to Think About...

"It is said that it is far more difficult to hold and maintain leadership than it is to attain it. Success is a ruthless competitor for it flatters and nourishes our weaknesses and lulls us into complacency. We bask in the sunshine of accomplishment and lose the spirit of humility which helps us visualize all the factors which have contributed to our success. We are apt to forget that we are only one of a team, that in unity there is strength and that we are strong only as long as each unit in our organization functions with precision."
—Samuel Tilden

The quote above aligns with what Jim Collins calls a Level 5 Executive: "Builds enduring greatness through a paradoxical combination of personal humility plus professional will."* *Are you this kind of leader?*
*"Level 5 Leadership: The Triumph of Humility and Fierce Resolve" HBR OnPoint © 2001.

Leading with Humility

Many seem to think that leadership and humility are oxymoronic. On the contrary, a true leader, a Legacy Leader®, MUST lead with humility. There is no option. Some people think leadership means ruling over a kingdom of serfs—slaves to their commands. Command and Control leadership doesn't work anymore. Albert Einstein eloquently stated: **"The high destiny of the individual is to serve rather than rule."** The same is true for the leader. While we can "take" pride in our work, being pride-full has no place in leadership. Consider this: **"Pride is concerned with WHO is right. Humility is concerned with WHAT is right."** *(Ezra Taft Benson)* This is a tremendously apt description of a Legacy Leader®.

- Would your team members describe your leadership style as one based on genuine humility? Describe what those team members might have to say about you in this regard. Are you satisfied with that? Do you need to make any changes? Can you honestly say that you lead with humility—real humility (not pretense; people know the difference, by the way!)—always?

ANSWERS

Unwavering Resolve to Accomplish Goals Through Others

Unwavering resolve is the "10" on the **commitment scale** of 1 to 10. This is not just a commitment to your work, but a resolve to accomplishing it as a team. It is a resolve to join forces as ONE unit instead of featuring a solo act seeking singular credit. It is your opportunity as a Legacy Leader® to build the leaders of tomorrow, while accomplishing the goals of today. This takes committed, unwavering resolve. Lao Tzu captured this concept. Consider this:

> "To lead people, walk beside them...
> As for the best leaders, the people do not notice their existence.
> The next best, the people honor and praise.
> The next, the people fear;
> And the next, the people hate.
> When the best leader's work is done the people say,
> 'We did it ourselves!'"

- Do you agree with this epigram above? Could this describe your leadership style? How? If not, why not, and how can you align your style more with this concept?

3:10 continued

TOP THREE

List your top 3 learnings, top 3 action plans, or top 3 personal reminders regarding this Critical Success Skill.

> "Sense shines with a double luster when it is set in humility. An able and yet humble man is a jewel worth a kingdom."
>
> —William Penn

The Influential Leader

What Does the Influential Leader Look Like?

Write down the name of the most influential person you know, or have known, and their characteristics. Use this diagram by placing labels to indicate the things that person knows (head), believes (heart) and does (hand and feet), etc.

Situational Story Development

Situational Storytelling: The influencing connection that keeps on giving!
The most impactful method of influence is through the ability to tell a persuasive story that connects both with the heart as well as the head, then translates to the hands and feet!

FROM: "I think I connect well with people."
TO: "I've been told I work well with people and in my most recent positions, it was a good thing I did! I inherited a creative team that didn't get along well at all. In fact, they couldn't seem to agree on anything. So, I met with the leaders of each group to discuss their objectives, problems, and desires. Then, after I spent some time sorting out what I heard in those meetings and drew some conclusions, I brought the group leaders together and shared my conclusions. To everyone's surprise, they all agreed with me. After some nervous laughter, camaraderie started to develop and the group leaders continued to meet on a regular basis. Today, they are the smoothest operating team in the organization."
From: Lions Don't Need To Roar by D.A. Benton

Components of an Inspiring Story

How To Tell a Story To Make a Connection
1. Draw from your own experiences.
2. Constantly add to your personal story collection.
3. Keep a file of stories.
4. Use descriptions.
5. Be personal.
6. Vary the length of your anecdotes and make sure any story you tell gets to its point quickly.
7. Inject humor whenever and wherever you can.

Seven Elements of Your Story
1. Introduction and setting of characters
2. Explanation of state of affairs
3. Initiating event: A situation
4. Emotional response OR statement of goal by the protagonist
5. Complicating actions
6. An outcome
7. Reactions to the outcome

For the exercise, choose one of the five Best Practices, and build a story (using the above guidelines) from your own experience to illustrate the concepts of this Best Practice. Use the lined pages to capture your story in bullet format, so you can memorize and share easily with others. (You may also wish to do this with all 5 Best Practices.

My story to share will illustrate:
- Best Practice 1: Holder of Vision and Values™
- Best Practice 2: Creator of Collaboration and Innovation™
- Best Practice 3: Influencer of Inspiration and Leadership™
- Best Practice 4: Advocator of Differences and Community™
- Best Practice 5: Calibrator of Responsibility and Accountability™

Situational Storytelling Exercise Notes

Situational Storytelling Exercise Notes

Situational Storytelling Worksheet
Stories to Illustrate Legacy Leadership

One Story (or example) that illuminates my understanding of Legacy Leadership®:

My story to demonstrate Best Practice 1 – Holder of Vision and Values™:

My story to demonstrate Best Practice 2 – Creator of Collaboration and Innovation™:

My story to demonstrate Best Practice 3 – Influencer of Inspiration and Leadership™:

My story to demonstrate Best Practice 4–Advocator of Differences and Community™:

My story to demonstrate Best Practice 5–Calibrator of Accountability and Responsibility™:

How I will incorporate Storytelling as a powerful leadership tool:

How I will inspire other Leaders to model Storytelling as a powerful leadership tool:

Situational Storytelling Notes

Best Practice 3

Influencer of Inspiration and Leadership™

Best Practice 3 Application Notes

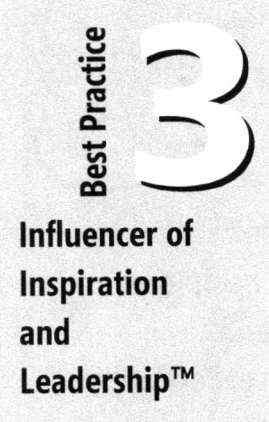

Best Practice 3
Influencer of Inspiration and Leadership™

Best Practice 3 Application Notes

Best Practice 4

Advocator of Differences and Community™

WHERE ARE YOU NOW?

Take a current snapshot of your leadership skills and competencies for this Best Practice right now. A sample scoring sheet is shown below. The assessment for BP4 is found on the next page.

Instructions for Completion

For each Best Practice there is a set of ten descriptive statements. YOU ARE ASKED TO PROVIDE A RATING FOR **TWO QUESTIONS** FOR EACH STATEMENT (referred to as a "dual rating assessment"):

PERFORMANCE: How often **do I exhibit** this stated behavior/attitude?
EXPECTATIONS: How often is this stated behavior/attitude **expected to occur** in my position?

Read each statement carefully, and honestly rate yourself on a scale of 1 to 5 as follows:
- *This statement describes my actual current behavior/attitude (PERFORMANCE):*
- *The statement describes how often this behavior/attitude should occur (EXPECTATIONS):*
    1—Not At All
    2—Occasionally
    3—On Average
    4—Frequently
    5—Consistently

Rate yourself for BOTH Performance and Expectations using this scale.
After you have rated each statement, total each column under each of the two sets of responses (Performance and Expectations) and place the total score for each of the five columns in the blanks provided. Then add the column score total across from left to right for a total score for each set of ratings on each Best Practice. Graph your responses.

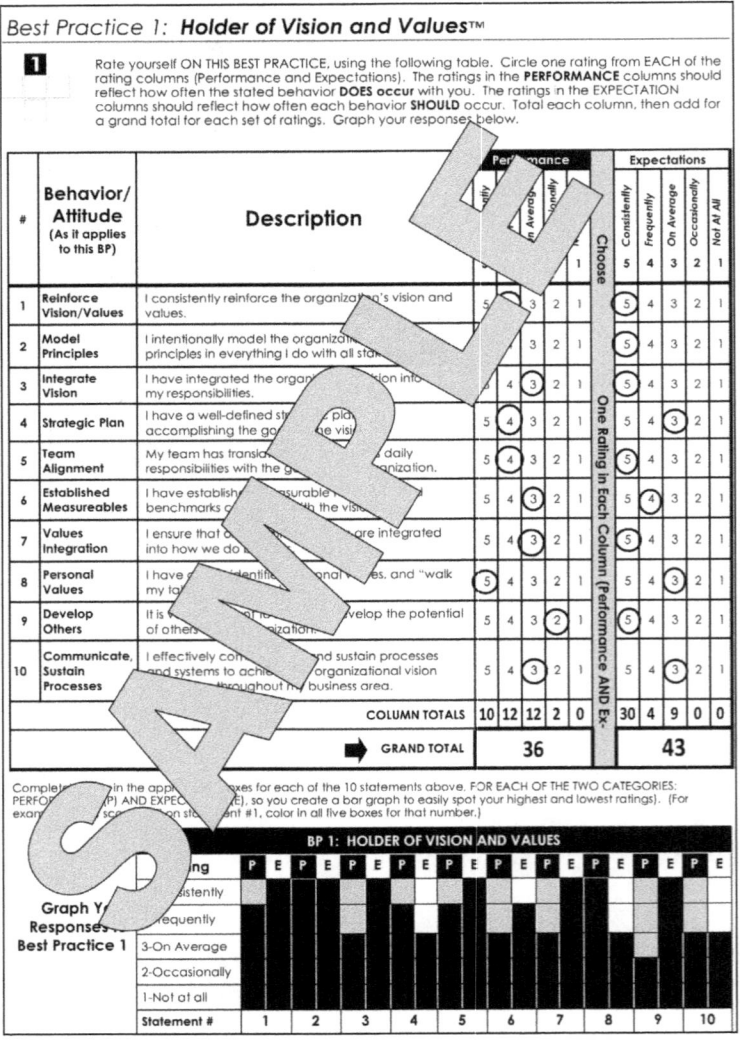

Best Practice 4: **Advocator of Differences and Community**™

Rate yourself ON THIS BEST PRACTICE, using the following table. Circle one rating from EACH of the rating columns (Performance and Expectations). The ratings in the **PERFORMANCE** columns should reflect how often the stated behavior **DOES occur** with you. The ratings in the EXPECTATION columns should reflect how often each behavior **SHOULD** occur. Total each column, then add for a grand total for each set of ratings. Graph your responses below.

#	Behavior/ Attitude (As it applies to this BP)	Description	Performance Consistently 5	Frequently 4	On Average 3	Occasionally 2	Not At All 1		Expectations Consistently 5	Frequently 4	On Average 3	Occasionally 2	Not At All 1
1	Ready Advocate	I am able to take a stand for a person, practice, or cause.	5	4	3	2	1		5	4	3	2	1
2	Mentor for Visibility	I constantly raise the visibility of individuals by mentoring and developing them.	5	4	3	2	1	Choose One Rating in Each Column (Performance AND Expectations)	5	4	3	2	1
3	Strengths-Based Culture	I am an advocate for a strengths-based culture where everyone works from their strengths.	5	4	3	2	1		5	4	3	2	1
4	Connoisseur of Talent	I am a connoisseur of talent, recognizing, valuing and utilizing the best each person has to offer.	5	4	3	2	1		5	4	3	2	1
5	Team Diversity	I insist on having teams of individuals with diverse approaches and capabilities.	5	4	3	2	1		5	4	3	2	1
6	Cross-Functional Opportunities	I look for cross-functional opportunities where unique talent can be developed.	5	4	3	2	1		5	4	3	2	1
7	Inter-Department Collaboration	I promote inter-departmental collaboration rather than "silo" orientation.	5	4	3	2	1		5	4	3	2	1
8	Consider Greater Community	I consider the impact of actions on the greater community beyond organizational boundaries.	5	4	3	2	1		5	4	3	2	1
9	Internal-External Communication	I have ongoing dialogue and involvement with internal and external communities.	5	4	3	2	1		5	4	3	2	1
10	United Inclusive Environment	I promote an inclusive environment that unites towards a common focus.	5	4	3	2	1		5	4	3	2	1
		COLUMN TOTALS											
		➡ **GRAND TOTAL**											

Completely color in the appropriate boxes for each of the 10 statements above, FOR EACH OF THE TWO CATEGORIES: PERFORMANCE (P) AND EXPECTATION (E), so you create a bar graph to easily spot your highest and lowest ratings). (For example, if you scored "5" on statement #1, color in all five boxes for that number.)

Graph Your Responses to Best Practice 4

BP 4: ADVOCATOR OF DIFFERENCES AND COMMUNITY™																				
Rating	P	E	P	E	P	E	P	E	P	E	P	E	P	E	P	E	P	E	P	E
5-Consistently																				
4-Frequently																				
3-On Average																				
2-Occasionally																				
1-Not at all																				
Statement #	1		2		3		4		5		6		7		8		9		10	

APPLY THE BASICS

Critical Success Skills: Core Competencies

Legacy Leaders acknowledge the importance and benefit of differences, and have an openness to diverse perspectives. They work hard to remove labels and prejudices, overcome comfort zones, and eliminate "rubber stamp" and "cookie cutter" mentality. Becoming a successful advocator of differences and community requires a keen desire to know others as people, not mere resources, and an understanding that when one grows and succeeds, all do. Advocating differences develops a passion for learning and discovery that unites these differences into community process instead of personal agenda. The ten critical success skills for this Legacy Practice serve to generate a team-building environment that tears down personal, departmental or organizational "walls" or silos, and fabricates a healthy culture based on understanding the community strength and ultimate success afforded in differences.

1. Be able to take a stand for a person, practice or cause.
2. Constantly raise visibility of individuals by mentoring and developing them.
3. Advocate for a strengths-based culture.
4. Be a connoisseur of talent, recognizing, valuing and utilizing the best each person has to offer.
5. Insist on building teams with diverse approaches and capabilities.
6. Look for and create cross-functional opportunities to develop unique talent.
7. Promote inter-departmental collaboration, rather than "silo" orientation.
8. Consider impact of actions on greater community (beyond organization).
9. Maintain ongoing dialogue/involvement with internal/external communities.
10. Promote inclusive environment to unite toward common focus.

Essence: *Being* a Legacy Leader
BE-Attitudes of an Advocator of Differences and Community

Great leaders who successfully apply this Legacy Practice will have a number of attitudes, traits and characteristics which allow them to fully advocate for differences and community. We could include such things as partnership-oriented, non-territorial, sharing, an enabler, and a promoter. These attitudes are all necessary. For leaders to truly live their legacy in this practice, however, there are some foundational BE-attitudes necessary to elevate their leadership from significance to legacy. We have listed the features we consider the Top Five BE-attitudes for your consideration in this Legacy Practice. These are not listed in any order of importance. Brief descriptions follow.

A Legacy Leader, an Advocator of Differences and Community, IS:

1. **A Champion**
2. **Inclusive/Uniter**
3. **Community-Minded**
4. **Discerning**
5. **Expectant** (Sense of Expectancy)

☐ **A Champion**
☐ **Inclusive/Uniter**
☐ **Community-Minded**
☐ **Discerning**
☐ **Expectant**

1. A Champion

This person is a ready advocate for individuals, or causes. They are natural encouragers, supporters, defenders and upholders. These leaders are others-centered, always seeking opportunities to champion people and issues worthy of support. These people are, however, careful and thoughtful in this support, taking a stand only after discerning whether or not people or issues align with their values.

2. Inclusive/A Uniter

This person has a natural or practiced ability to unite people in teams, for causes, to achieve results and to develop community. This inclusiveness always seeks uniquenesses and strengths to add to the overall vigor of the community, and has the ability to recognize value in diversity where others may not.

3. Community-Minded

This person is able to identify common denominators and uniting factors in groups, and uses these commonalities to build teams of people with shared goals. These leaders understand that the greatest accomplishments are the result of working together as a whole, where every individual is valued and recognized.

4. Discerning

This person has either an inherent or cultivated ability to make solid decisions and judgments based on sound consideration of all information available. He or she is able to distinguish between close and seemingly similar things for the betterment of self and others. These leaders are able to determine and recognize individual gifts, strengths and uniquenesses. This ability allows them to build strong diverse teams.

5. Expectant (Sense of Expectancy)

This person is always expecting results, anticipating goals to be met and people to work together to achieve common objectives. This expectancy is modeled to others who then sense, understand and therefore work toward stated goals, often with a renewed focus or urgency. These leaders have a clear sense of vision, strategies and ultimate purpose for being in community, on which their expectancy is based.

BE-ATTITUDE SELF ASSESSMENT

How developed is your core being for becoming a Legacy Leader in this Legacy Practice? After reading the descriptions of these BE-Attitudes above, rate yourself *(circle one)* on the following scale, then go on to the steps and questions that follow.

	BE-ATTITUDES of an Advocator of Differences and Community	RATING: 5=all the time, 0=not at all
1	I am a champion.	5 4 3 2 1 0
2	I am inclusive, a uniter.	5 4 3 2 1 0
3	I am community-minded.	5 4 3 2 1 0
4	I am discerning.	5 4 3 2 1 0
5	I am expectant (have a sense of expectation).	5 4 3 2 1 0

Where do your ratings fall? How many 5's? Any 2's or below? Any zeros? Here are some suggestions for building the core being of an Influencer of Inspiration and Leadership.

1. **Choose your two highest ratings**. Determine how you can leverage these strengths to be even more effective in developing and living your leadership legacy. **Also choose two of your lowest** rating attitudes to be your "work on" areas for improvement. Use the questions below to build your BE-attitudes.

2. **Think of someone you know to be this**, to have this attitude, for each of the two areas you selected for improvement. For example, if you scored yourself low in being seamless in your behavior in all places, who do you know whose behavior *is* seamless (past or present)? Identify one person for each of the areas you want to develop and do the following exercises. Write the attitudes and person's name here:

   ATTITUDE   **PERSON I KNOW WHO DISPLAYS THIS ATTITUDE**
   1.
   2.

   Consider the following for each attitude, and person listed:

   a. What does this person do that lets me, and others, know he or she is

   _____ (BE-Attitude)?

b. How can I emulate this behavior/attitude?

c. How will this behavior help me become a better leader? A Legacy Leader?

3. After completing the above steps, **make a commitment** to improve. Choose one of your "work on" attitudes each week, and focus on improving that attitude in all you think, do and speak. Practice these things for each BP you work on:

   a. Be aware of your behavior and thought processes during the week, as they pertain to that attitude.

   b. Create a mental reminder that will alert you to old behavior and thought patterns you want to change.

   c. When you are alerted to old behavior and thought patterns, change them immediately, if possible. If not, use that experience to help remind you in the future. Consider what triggered this old behavior or attitude, and how you can respond differently in the future.

   d. Evaluate your week for progress and determine how you can improve this attitude next week.

   e. The following week, add another "work on" attitude as your focus, without neglecting the first one.

   f. Keep doing this until you notice a definite change (improvement), so that your improved attitude has become part of you, part of your core being as a Legacy Leader. Chances are if *you* notice an improvement, others will as well.

   g. If journaling is familiar and comfortable for you, consider keeping track of your BE-Attitude development. Brush away discouragement if things don't change immediately. They will, especially if this is the way you want to be. Sometimes we just need to rethink or reframe how we think and do.

WRITE ANY COMMENTS BELOW YOU THINK MIGHT HELP YOU STRENGTHEN THESE BE-ATTITUDES...

NOTES

DRILL DOWNS
Best Practice 4

The following section includes drill down *(more targeted and focused)* opportunities for each of the ten critical success skills for Best Practice 4. You may wish to complete the ones you have determined you need to strengthen first, but in order to truly round out your competencies and skills in this best practice, it is best to complete them all.

Drill Down 4:1

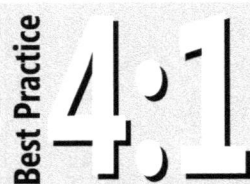

CRITICAL SUCCESS SKILL #1:

Be able to take a stand for a person, practice, or cause.

Advocator of Differences and Community™

Something to Think About...

"Perhaps you have heard the expression, "the person who stands for nothing will fall for anything." In order to genuinely lead, you must stand for something. You must be willing to commit yourself to certain beliefs, values and actions. Then you must be willing to make them public. This is risky, ...because when you make your positions visible, others will hold you much more accountable for them. Finally, you must then stay true to the stands you have taken. People will be watching you with a crooked eye to make sure that the actions you take are in line with the lofty or passionate words you have spoken."

"The Risk of Taking a Stand"
By Steve Coats,
In CEO Refresher

Do you take a stand for what (or who) you believe is right in your area of responsibility? What are the risks of doing this? Do you do it anyway? What are the results?

Taking a Stand

The dictionary defines taking a "stand" as adopting a position, adhering to a certain policy or attitude, and upholding, supporting and defending something or someone. In short, the person taking a stand becomes an ADVOCATE for a person, practice or cause.

Without the ability to take a stand, leadership fails and crumbles at the first sign of trouble. Abraham Lincoln, in his usual simple but profound manner, said the following:

"Stand with anybody that stands right, stand with him while he is right and part with him when he goes wrong."

Good advice for anyone, especially the leader. There are three basic components that can be derived from President Lincoln's simple statement:

1. Always stand FOR RIGHT
2. Always stand WITH THOSE who stand for right
3. Do NOT STAND for what is NOT right

Ad-vō-cāte *(v)*
1. To support or urge by argument; recommend publicly
2. To defend a cause or person
3. To plead, or intercede on behalf of a cause or person

The leader must first know WHAT is right. He or she must be completely on top of all business situations to know when a practice or cause is right for the organization, for the strategic vision or plan, AND whether it is right ethically and morally—and personally. If you know it is right, how will you advocate for it? What will you do if it is threatened in any way?

ANSWERS

The leader must make a commitment also to stand with others who are right, whether they are advocating for the person, or for a cause, practice or action of the person. The leader may also find him or herself advocating for SELF, rather than someone else. Both positions are common in business, and the ability to take this stand is necessary for effective leadership. How do you do this?

And, perhaps most importantly, the leader must know when to NOT stand with or for a person, practice or cause that is NOT right. Do you know the difference? Do you have this kind of wisdom and discernment? Do you act on it consistently?

Taking a stand in business applications also involves standing firm for certain policies, procedures, vision, or practices that you as leader think are right. How do you do this? How do you know when to NOT stand, or to change your stand? Have you identified the risks? Are you willing to take them? Do you have the courage?

- Are you a ready advocate? Do you always advocate or take a stand for what is right?

- What person, situation, practice or cause exists in your life (business or otherwise) right now that you should take a stand for? Have you? How? If not, why not and what can you do about it?

- Are you able to take a stand AGAINST what is NOT right? Explain.

4:1 continued

TOP THREE

List your top 3 learnings, top 3 action plans, or top 3 personal reminders regarding this Critical Success Skill.

Drill Down 4:2

Best Practice 4:2

CRITICAL SUCCESS SKILL #2:
Constantly raise the visibility of individuals by mentoring and developing them.

Advocator of Differences and Community™

Mentoring and Developing

Mentoring is a popular buzz word in today's leadership circles. Most of the time the word elicits visions of organizational programs, training and structured systems for mentoring. These programs are very important for many reasons. Consider this: **"The case for mentoring in organizations is now more compelling than ever. It is clear that mentoring supports the retention, development and engagement of today's workforce. It is a direct link to an organization's productivity and, ultimately, profitability. No one really needs to be convinced as to what a powerful and dynamic process mentoring can be for both employees and organizations. It has the potential to elevate corporate dialogue from the mundane to the truly transformational."** *(Beverley Kaye, in "Fast Track Mentoring: Sparking Ideas for Collaborative Conversations" adapted from "Power Mentoring™").* Yes, everyone knows mentoring programs are powerful tools within organizations.

In this Critical Success Skill, for this Best Practice, however, **mentoring applies not to just a program, but to an ATTITUDE**. Whether or not an officially sanctioned mentoring program exists within the organization, a leader's attitude should always be one of mentor, seeking opportunities to develop others and raise their visibility.

Something to Think About...

"Business Week reports that over 35% of employees who are not being mentored within 12 months of being hired, are actively looking for a job."

—Beverly Kaye

Do you approach your leadership with a mentoring attitude? What are the results?

★ ANSWERS

- Spend some time considering your mentoring skills and attitude with your current team members. Are you leading as a mentor now, with your team members? If not, who should you mentor?

Team member you are, or should be, mentoring now	For what purpose, or reason(s)?	What do/can you do, to mentor this person (specific actions)	What development opportunities do/can you provide?	How do/can you raise this person's visibility?

- What does it mean to you to be a leader-mentor?

4:2 continued

TOP THREE

List your top 3 learnings, top 3 action plans, or top 3 personal reminders regarding this Critical Success Skill.

Drill Down 4:3

Best Practice 4:3

CRITICAL SUCCESS SKILL #3:
Be an advocate for a strengths-based culture where everyone works from their strengths.

Advocator of Differences and Community™

Something to Think About...

"Quality is never an accident; it is always the result of high intention, sincere effort, intelligent direction and skillful execution; it represents the wise choice of many alternatives."

—Willa A. Foster

A strengths-based culture yields quality and quantity. It, too, "represents the wise choice of many alternatives." Have you made wise choices regarding the utilization of the strengths of your team members in your area of responsibility?

Strengths-Based Culture

"The best way to develop people and net the greatest return on investment in their growth is to identify their talents, then help them add the skills and knowledge that build strengths—the ability to provide consistent, near-perfect performance." *(The Gallup Organization)*

A "strengths-based culture" is built any number of ways, but the essence is basically to identify the strengths of your workers and align them with the needed outcomes for your area of responsibility. The focus is always on strengths. We all know it is good business to have the right fit for employees and desired outcomes. There are many excellent programs available to guide you through the steps of doing this. That is not our purpose.

The focus of this CSS is to be sure that you are actively ADVOCATING, promoting and encouraging, building and preserving this culture. DO you know the strengths of your individual team members? DO you have them in the right position? ARE they working from their strengths? Do you measure strengths and match to desired results? This is not a one-time event; it is an ongoing diligence where you become highly in tune with your team members, knowing their strengths and continuing to assign work or place them into positions where their strengths shine and they achieve the desired outcomes. As positions or tasks change, this balance is altered. Do you check this? Can you, at any given time, easily state the strengths of each of your team members, and say with assurance, that each one is in the right

★ ANSWERS

place, doing the right thing, working from their strengths? THIS is what this CSS is about. Employees consistently working from their strengths is an intentional design, requiring effort, intelligent direction and skillful execution, as the quote in the sidebar indicates.

- What are you doing today to know the strengths of your team members? DO you know them?

- Are they all working from their strengths? If not, what can you do about it?

- Are desired outcomes the result?

- What will you commit to doing to advocate for this strengths-based culture? Continually?

- Do you know your own strengths? Are YOU working from your strengths? If not, how can this be corrected?

4:3 continued

TOP THREE

List your top 3 learnings, top 3 action plans, or top 3 personal reminders regarding this Critical Success Skill.

CAUTION!

Like any good idea, the concept of a strengths-based culture can be taken to the extreme, out of balance. Be careful of the directives of some to disregard your weaknesses and pour all your efforts into developing strengths. Avoid the temptation to cover up unacceptable or weak performance with attention only to strengths. While it is true that at times efforts to upgrade weaknesses in individuals is a futile and frustrating effort, attention to strengths only should never be a cover for tolerance of unacceptable performance, which may or may not be due to a person's "weaknesses." Don't use this as a "cop-out" for excellence!

Drill Down 4:4

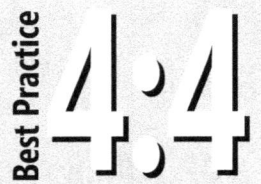

Best Practice 4:4

CRITICAL SUCCESS SKILL #4:
Be a connoisseur of talent, recognizing, valuing and utilizing the best each person has to offer.

Advocator of Differences and Community™

A "Connoisseur of Talent"

Best Practice 4 is about advocating for differences and promoting those differences into strong community for successful outcomes. The Critical Success Skills associated with BP4 delineate the "how" of this practice, and build on each other. For example, CSS3, covered in the last Drill Down, states, "Be an advocate for a strengths-based culture where everyone works from their strengths." CSS4, the subject of this exercise, provides the HOW.

> **CONNOISSEUR**
> 1. A person competent to pass critical judgments in an art or in matters of taste;
> 2. A discerning judge of the best in any field.

The Consortium for Research on Emotional Intelligence in Organizations (www.eiconsortium.org) has published "The Emotional Competence Framework," distilled from many sources on Emotional Intelligence. Under the heading "Social Competence" they state:

Leveraging diversity: Cultivating opportunities through diverse people. People with this competence:

- Respect and relate well to people from varied backgrounds
- Understand diverse worldviews and are sensitive to group differences
- See diversity as opportunity, creating an environment where diverse people can thrive
- Challenge bias and intolerance

Something to Think About...

"There is something that is much more scarce, something rarer than ability. It is the ability to recognize ability."

—Robert Half

We've seen this quote many times before, but it is still around because it is very powerful and very true. Do you have this ability to recognize ability? If so, what do you do with it? How do you leverage it for successful attainment of goals?

★ ANSWERS

Most will interpret those words as relating to the broad topic of "diversity" which is most often thought to be about cultural or ethnic backgrounds or personal preferences. Legacy Leadership broadens this topic to include diversity in every area, including talent and strengths. It is easy to make statements like *"see diversity as opportunity, creating an environment where diverse people can thrive."* Okay, good. But exactly HOW do you do that? If you are advocating for differences and diversity in talents and strengths, you do it by becoming a CONNOISSEUR OF TALENT.

We think of a "connoisseur" usually in terms of gourmet food or the fine arts. This person has a cultivated sense of the best. So does a Legacy Leader. He or she has a cultivated sense of the best in talent and strengths. A connoisseur becomes a connoisseur by practice, not by accident. Careful and deliberate observation combined with developed discernment and testing earn the connoisseur this title. A Legacy Leader® takes this one step further. Being a connoisseur generally implies recognition. Being a Legacy Leader® practicing Best Practice 4 implies not only recognizing, but also valuing and utilizing.

- Have you cultivated your ability to recognize talent? How? Provide an example.

- How do you VALUE this talent? Be specific.

- How do you UTILIZE this talent? Be specific.

- What opportunities exist right now in your area to practice being a connoisseur of talent?

4:4 continued

TOP THREE

List your top 3 learnings, top 3 action plans, or top 3 personal reminders regarding this Critical Success Skill.

Drill Down 4:5

Best Practice 4:5

CRITICAL SUCCESS SKILL #5:
Insist on having teams of individuals with diverse approaches and capabilities.

Advocator of Differences and Community™

Teams with Diverse Approaches and Capabilities

We have already stated that this Best Practice expands the commonly interpreted concept of DIVERSITY. Yes, we advocate for diversity in the workplace, and all that those words imply regarding cultural, ethnic and personal differences. But having optimally functioning and producing teams of individuals in business means insisting on diversity on many levels. These are just some of the diversities and differences that contribute to high functioning teams:

- Cultural and ethnic backgrounds
- Experiences
- Perspectives
- Personality
- Styles

There are many other kinds of diversity that can be valued in a team environment. You can add to this list those appropriate for your area. As you develop your teams, consider this: **"Never hire or promote in your own image. It is foolish to replicate your strength and idiotic to replicate your weakness. It is essential to employ, trust, and reward those whose perspective, ability, and judgment are radically different from yours. It is also, rare, for it requires uncommon humility, tolerance, and wisdom."** *(Dee W. Hock)*

An organization may make deliberate attempts at hiring individuals with diversity, giving their HR departments guidelines and "quotas." That is only a weak first step. These diverse people must then be shaped into

Something to Think About...

"If everyone is thinking alike, then somebody isn't thinking."

General George S. Patton

How does your team measure up against this statement? Do all of your team members think alike? Are you all cut "from the same mold?" What value could be derived from diversity in thought, as well as every other area?

 ANSWERS

collaborative teams which value, respect and draw collective community strength from this diversity. This is where many organizations fail—not at being diverse, but in working together in that diversity. For some reason, diversity is a subject that many like to sweep under the corporate carpet. Instead, we should be exploring and exalting diversity, and putting it to work.

In **"Why Should Anyone Be Led By You?"** authors Robert Goffee and Gareth Jones write about four "unexpected" qualities of inspirational leaders. This article states that good leaders **"...reveal their differences...capitalize on what's unique about themselves..."** and "selectively show their weaknesses." *(Harvard Business Review)* It's time to actually POINT OUT differences, discuss uniquenesses, then work together to build them into a strong collaborative community.

- Describe your current team. What are team members' individual differences?

- How could this team be more diverse, and how would that diversity lend to its strength?

- Do you honestly acknowledge differences and recognize the value of diversity? Do you put it to work for you? How?

4:5 continued

TOP THREE

List your top 3 learnings, top 3 action plans, or top 3 personal reminders regarding this Critical Success Skill.

"Everyone is ignorant, only on different subjects."
—Will Rogers

Drill Down 4:6

Best Practice 4:6

CRITICAL SUCCESS SKILL #6:
Look for cross-functional opportunities where unique talent can be developed.

Developing Unique Talent through Cross Functional Opportunities

Advocator of Differences and Community™

Recognizing strengths, becoming a connoisseur of talent and advocating for a strengths-based culture is not limited to functional, team or departmental boundaries. To make the most of any organization's greatest resource—its people—these invisible lines of demarcation need to be crossed.

Consider this: **"The hardest mindset to alter is the belief that capital is the critical strategic resource to be managed. Today, there is a surplus of capital chasing a scarcity of talented, knowledgeable people…Scarce knowledge and expertise cannot be accumulated at the top, but it resides within individuals at all levels. Senior managers must nurture individual expertise and initiative and then leverage it through cross-unit sharing. Part of their role will be to create a sense of purpose and inject meaning into individual effort."** (C. A. Bartlett and S. Ghoshal in *"Building Competitive Advantage Through People,"* Sloan Management Review)

Something to Think About…

"Production is not the application of tools to materials, but logic to work."

—*Peter Drucker*

Diversity, differences of all sorts, includes more than the above-stated "expertise and knowledge." We have already discussed the variety of differences that should be promoted within an organization and within a team. This promotion should extend across functions, across teams and across departments—even across seniority levels, if appropriate. Do you want your organization to function better, as well as it can? Are you willing to be realistic, practical and smart about who does what, regardless of common "taboos?" Are you willing to take risks to develop talent by stepping over lines? Really?

This Critical Success Skill involves observation, recognition, common sense (logic!) and risk. It is smarter to apply logic to the work process by seeking cross-functional opportunities (and other boundaries to cross) to develop talent and work more efficiently. Do you do this? How? What are the risks? Do you take those risks?

ANSWERS

If Susan has proven herself to be a good organizer, why is John doing that job? If John has exhibited observable negotiating skills, why is he still organizing while Alex is struggling in negotiation functions? Some of this is just good old fashioned common sense (a scarcity in itself these days, and not so common). Some of this is having the fortitude to cross previously "untouchable" and traditionally hands-off boundaries. It takes courage to buck the "that's always the way we've done it" syndrome by advocating development of your people across traditional lines.

- Have you honestly attempted to identify skills, competencies, strengths and talents in those around you, not only within your area of responsibility, but in other areas? Could you identify at least one strength in each person you work with? How about one "budding" unique talent in each?

- Are these people currently working in places and on projects where those strengths and unique talents are showcased and developed? How, or why not? What can you do about it?

- If you ignored functions, ignored teams, ignored departments and ignored seniority, how would you re-assign these people? Who would be doing what and why? Now, are there any valid reasons why you CAN'T do this? (There may be some!)

- What first steps can you take to develop talent through cross-functional opportunities?

4:6 continued

TOP THREE

List your top 3 learnings, top 3 action plans, or top 3 personal reminders regarding this Critical Success Skill.

Drill Down 4:7

Best Practice 4:7

CRITICAL SUCCESS SKILL #7:
Promote inter-departmental collaboration rather than "silo" orientation.

Advocator of Differences and Community™

Something to Think About...

"Any man who knows all the answers most likely misunderstood the questions."
—*Unknown*

Work groups, teams, departments and other organizational clusters or collectives quite often work as busy little bees in their designated hives, loyal to and aware only of their work, their function or their role—their hive. It is easy to slip into the "self-contained" have-all-the-answers mode. NO one, no department has all the answers. How could your work area benefit from more inter-department collaboration?

Cross-Department Collaboration vs. Silo Operation

An organization is a whole made up of many parts. These parts take the form of departments, teams, project groups, leadership levels and many other area or function designations. In order for the whole to function properly, each part must collaborate wholly with the others. If not, the old adage becomes the sad by-line: "the left hand doesn't know what the right hand is doing." If this is true, if groups or teams or even individuals work as "silos" (unattached and independent), confusion, chaos and tumbling profits reign.

A Legacy Leader seeks opportunity for cross-department or inter-department collaboration, lines of communication, and information/talent sharing conduits. Milton Berle said **"if opportunity doesn't knock—build a door."** Inter-departmental collaboration requires a bridge. A door can be shut. Build a bridge instead, allowing free access between departments, areas or teams. This bridge is built on trust, and is made strong by the resulting diversity it promotes. The parts make a whole community when the bridge of collaboration spans the gaps between parts.

It is, of course, much easier to be a silo than a bridge. Marshall Goldsmith, in an article titled *"Building Partnerships Inside and Outside the Organization"* (from "Partnering: The New Face of Leadership") wrote: **"Almost every high-potential leader we interviewed believed that the leader of the future would need to be far more skilled than the leader of the past. In many ways the "old world" was simpler....Being able to work in a "silo" is a lot simpler than having to build**

★ ANSWERS

partnerships with peers across the organization." Building and maintaining bridges between departments, peers or other organizational groups or individuals is hard work, time consuming and challenging. But well worth the effort. Are you up to that?

- What collaborative bridges between departments in your area of responsibility exist right now? How were they built, and how are they maintained?

- What benefits to the organization as a whole, and to your area as a part, are gained as a result of this collaboration?

- What differences and diversity strengthen the organization because of these bridges? How do they benefit you and the organization?

- What bridges still need to be built? What departments should you be building a bridge to? How can you collaborate together, yet still function within your area as you should? How can new inter-department collaboration help the organization reach its vision and goals faster, better? Make a list here of at least 3 new bridges that would benefit your department. How will you facilitate building them? What will it look like? What is your plan to do this?

    1.
    2.
    3.

4:7 continued

TOP THREE

List your top 3 learnings, top 3 action plans, or top 3 personal reminders regarding this Critical Success Skill.

Drill Down 4:8

Best Practice 4:8

Advocator of Differences and Community™

Something to Think About…

"The 4-way test of the things we think, say or do..
1) Is it the truth?
2) Is it fair to all concerned?
3) Will it build good will and better relationships?
4) Will it be beneficial to all concerned?"

—Rotary International Motto

This motto contains a great reminder of the need to consider the impact of our actions on others. We are all connected, and even more so in business. What other questions should be asked? What questions or considerations are particularly appropriate and relevant for your area of responsibility?

CRITICAL SUCCESS SKILL #8:
Consider the impact of actions on the greater community, beyond organizational boundaries.

The "Greater Community" and You

What exactly is this "greater community?" The phrase "organizational boundaries" includes many smaller communities such as other departments, teams, management and leadership levels—even individuals. These are intra-organizational boundaries. Extra-organizational boundaries include vendors, subcontractors, other service providers, local community groups or concerns. And one group quite often lost in the shuffle—the customer! To comprehend the scope of the greater community, unfold those unwieldy organizational charts and then start tracing and tracking outward, beyond the company. Exactly who and what does your organization touch now—and will in the future?

John Maxwell said, **"The greatest mistake we make is living in constant fear that we will make one."** This Critical Success Skill is perhaps one of the best ways to eliminate, or at least greatly reduce, that fear. When the impact of an organization's, or an individual leader's, actions are carefully considered, tracking them within and as far out beyond the organization as possible, the chances that these actions will be mistakes is slim.

Here's a good exercise to give you a picture of your greater community. Draw a little box in the center of a page and label it with you and your area of responsibility (two blank pages follow for this exercise). Around this center box draw more boxes to indicate all the other departments, areas, teams, etc. within your organization. Draw lines to show your inter-dependence. Add any other entities or communities that show inter-department impact. Draw a large circle around all of these boxes—what is inside represents the organization. Now draw more boxes on the outside of the big circle. These represent all those groups/individuals that your organization touches. Label them, and show who they touch, and so on. It is a dramatic way to get a feel for who and what needs to be considered when you and your organization are about to take certain actions.

ANSWERS

If you continue this exercise to show the "ripple" effects of other people and groups on one another, coming from you (the center), it is also an eye-opening representation of your Legacy as a leader.

Use the pages that follow for your community drawing, then summarize it in the space below.

4:8 continued

TOP THREE

List your top 3 learnings, top 3 action plans, or top 3 personal reminders regarding this Critical Success Skill.

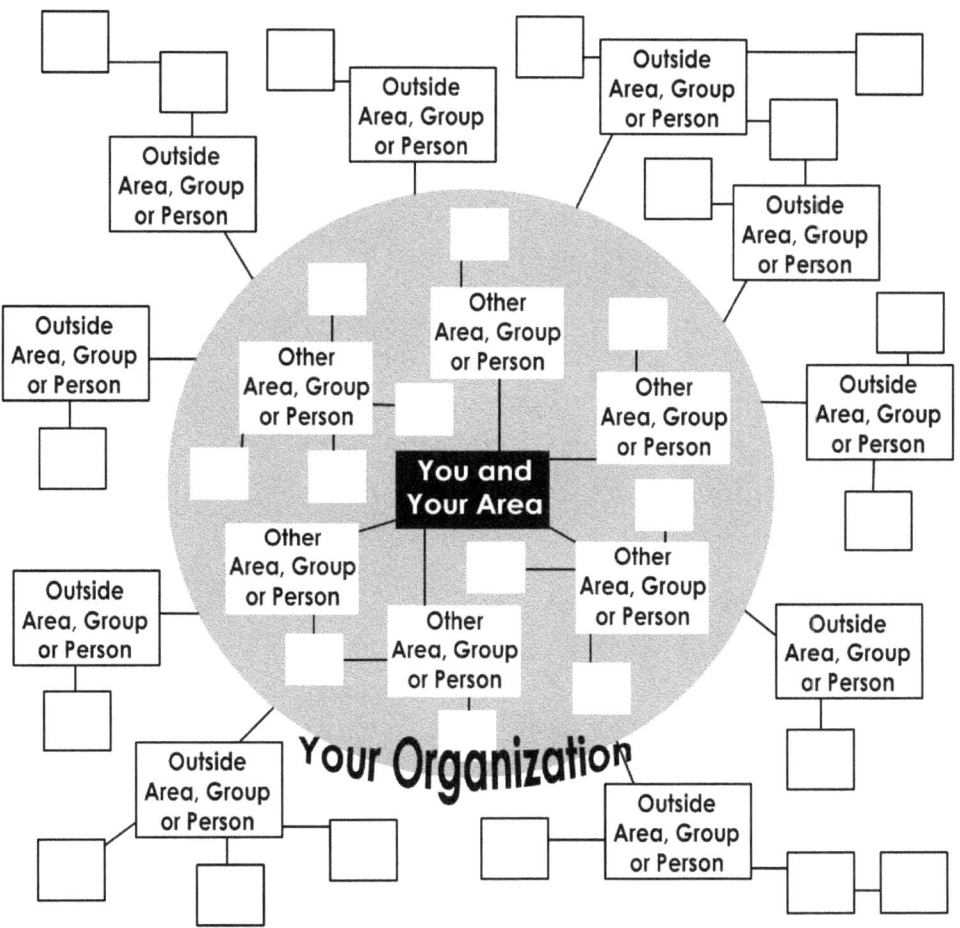

Are you getting the picture? Save your drawing and refer to it as you consider the impact of your actions on the greater community.

Drill Down 4:8 (continued)

Your "Greater Community" Drawing

Drill Down 4:9

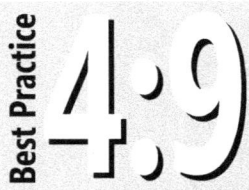

CRITICAL SUCCESS SKILL #9:
Maintain ongoing dialogue and involvement with internal and external communities.

Advocator of Differences and Community™

Partnering with All Communities

If you did the "Greater Community" exercise in the previous Drill Down, you will be well prepared for this one. If you have not taken the time to draw out and identify your internal and external "communities," stop right here and do it now.

If leaders are going to "Consider the impact of actions on the greater community, beyond organizational boundaries" (previous—Best Practice 4, Critical Success Skill #8), quite obviously they must first be able to identify that greater community. Then, in order to best assess the impact of actions, leaders must also have some established dialogue and involvement with these internal and external groups—SO THAT potential impacts can be fully known.

This is only one (albeit very important!) reason for these internal and external partnerships. There are many parts to a whole, both within organizations and without. The organization, as a whole, is part of an even greater whole. When all parts share information and involve one another, knowledge is transferred more quickly and efficiently, and the whole "machine" runs smoother, traveling in the same direction.

Dialogue and consistent communication is essential to community partnerships. Consider this: **"In most vital organizations, there is a common bond of interdependence, mutual interest, interlocking contributions, and simple joy. Part of the art of leadership is to see that this common bond is maintained**

Something to Think About...

"...building partnerships inside and outside the organization is going to become a requirement, not an option, for future leaders."

—Marshall Goldsmith

Do you agree with this statement? Why or why not? How relevant is it to your work now, and future work, in your area? What partnerships should you be developing now?

ANSWERS

and strengthened, a task certainly requiring good communication. Just as any relationship requires honest and open communication to stay healthy, so the relationships within corporations improve when information is shared accurately and freely." *(DePree, Leadership is an Art)*. This is true for relationships and partnerships outside the corporation as well. However, don't fall into the old trap that more is always better. The quantity of communication does not necessarily have any bearing on its quality. That old sage Yogi Berra put it eloquently: **"It was impossible to get a conversation going— everybody was talking too much."** What is communicated, how it is communicated, and when, are far more important than merely a dialogue for the sake of dialogue. That is "token talk" and doesn't serve any purpose. Communication between internal and external communities must be well planned, carefully constructed, and diligently maintained for quality and results.

- List your top 3 "greater community" groups WITHIN the organization. Describe the quality of your communication with these groups, and your level of involvement. Should it be better? How, and what will you do about it?

- If appropriate, do the same exercise for the top 3 groups/individuals OUTSIDE the organization.

- Run a "diagnostic" on ALL your internal and external communities. Are you regularly communicating, and adequately involved? How? What can you do better?

4:9
continued

TOP THREE

List your top 3 learnings, top 3 action plans, or top 3 personal reminders regarding this Critical Success Skill.

The new paradigm of strategy-making requires thinking in terms of whole systems ... seeing your organization as part of a wider economic ecosystem and environment ... start with an understanding of the big picture rather than of products and services.
—J. Moore

Drill Down 4:10

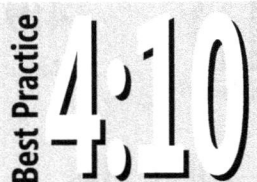

CRITICAL SUCCESS SKILL #10:

Promote an inclusive environment that unites toward a common focus.

Advocator of Differences and Community™

Promoting an Inclusive and Unified Environment for Success

In the past several Drill Downs in this Best Practice we have discussed differences and diversity of many kinds, as well as community and partnering. In this last Critical Success Skill for Best Practice 4 we have the final element of the formula:

**(Differences/diversity + collaborative community) X
(inclusive united environment) =
common focus » success**

Combine healthy differences to make broad diversity, add a collaborative community and multiply the whole thing by an inclusive united environment, shake it up with a strong advocate, and you get common focus, which encourages success. Simple formula—and it works. This formula only works, however, if all the elements are in place. Promoting differences and diversity only creates islands adrift in the community sea if the inclusive and united environment is missing.

The Right Stuff... "IT'S NOT ABOUT ME."

So where do you start? Just how do you build, then promote, this inclusive environment that is magnetized and polarized into common focus? Consider this: **"What we need to do is learn to work in the system, by which I mean that everybody, every team, every platform, every division, every component is there not for individual competitive profit or recognition, but for contribution to the system as a whole on a win-win basis."** *(W. Edwards Deming)*

Something to Think About...

"Dependent people need others to get what they want. Independent people can get what they want through their own efforts. Interdependent people combine their own efforts with the efforts of others to achieve their greatest success."
—Steven Covey

Are you dependent, independent or interdependent in your area of responsibility? How do you create and promote an inclusive environment that unites toward common focus?

★ ANSWERS

There are many practical actions that can be taken to promote an inclusive environment. You will find opportunities around every cubicle for this—if you're looking for them. But before these action steps can be taken, something much more difficult, and more foundational, must be in place—**THE RIGHT ATTITUDE**. YOUR attitude. It begins with you. Remember your "Greater Community" exercise (BP4-CSS8)? Your attitude dictates your words and actions and impacts everyone around you.

The attitude of a Legacy Leader, an Advocator of Differences and Community, is this: **"IT'S NOT ABOUT ME."** Can you imagine what your company could accomplish if everyone had this attitude? Sit back and watch the fences fall, the walls crumble and the bottom line soar.

Unfortunately, this attitude is very rare in the corporate jet stream—anywhere for that matter. Is it rare for you? Is it rare in your organization? It all starts with one. Are you the one? Once a leader adopts this attitude—humbly, honestly and not arrogantly acting a part—the rest of the steps toward an inclusive environment will be obvious. This leader will be alert to possibilities that bridge gaps, include all differences and parts, and generate a community-wide common focus.

- Rate your attitude on the "IT'S NOT ABOUT ME SCALE" and describe why you gave yourself this rating. Are you prepared to become a perfect "10?"

```
0    1    2    3    4    5    6    7    8    9    10
|----|----|----|----|----|----|----|----|----|----|
It's ALL                                        It's NOT
about me                                        about me
```

- List all the things you are currently doing to promote an inclusive environment. What else can you do?

4:10 continued

TOP THREE

List your top 3 learnings, top 3 action plans, or top 3 personal reminders regarding this Critical Success Skill.

Personal Work

For Your Own Leadership Position:

For Your Peer Team

1. Do you know the specific talents of your primary peer team? Can you list them here?

2. Are you able to easily listen to differing opinions without feeling threatened? Explain. (Be honest!)

3. Does your peer team have enough diversity of perspective in order to create innovative solutions? Explain a "yes" or "no" answer.

4. Is trust enhanced because of a feeling of community among the members? If not, what would it take to have this happen?

For Your Direct Reports

1. Is the information about your direct reports readily available to you?

2. Can you identify their strengths and diversities that contribute to your goals?

3. Have you actively drawn out the strengths of employees for the purpose of having them be completely engaged in their work and utilized fully? How? How can you do a better job of this? What reminders will you use?

Personal Work

Your current work situation in general...

Use this page to honestly evaluate your current work situation, both with peers, direct reports, customers and any other groups you work with. How can this Best Practice be utilized within these groups? Write a plan using bullet points to indicate how you can implement the Critical Success Skills of this Best Practice in your workplace, regardless of your position.

Best Practice 4

Advocator of Differences and Community™

Best Practice 4 Application Notes

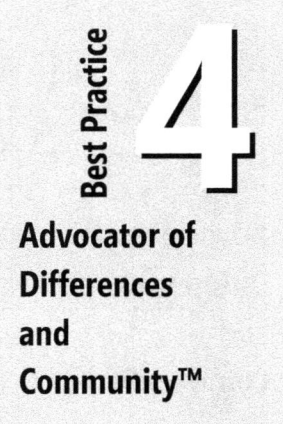

Best Practice 4 Application Notes

Advocator of Differences and Community™

Best Practice 5
Calibrator of Responsibility and Accountability™

WHERE ARE YOU NOW?

Take a current snapshot of your leadership skills and competencies for this Best Practice right now. A sample scoring sheet is shown below. The assessment for BP5 is found on the next page.

Instructions for Completion

For each Best Practice there is a set of ten descriptive statements. YOU ARE ASKED TO PROVIDE A RATING FOR **TWO QUESTIONS** FOR EACH STATEMENT (referred to as a "dual rating assessment"):

PERFORMANCE: How often **do I exhibit** this stated behavior/attitude?
EXPECTATIONS: How often is this stated behavior/attitude **expected to occur** in my position?

Read each statement carefully, and honestly rate yourself on a scale of 1 to 5 as follows:
- *This statement describes my actual current behavior/attitude (PERFORMANCE):*
- *The statement describes how often this behavior/attitude should occur (EXPECTATIONS):*

    1—Not At All
    2—Occasionally
    3—On Average
    4—Frequently
    5—Consistently

Rate yourself for BOTH Performance and Expectations using this scale.

After you have rated each statement, total each column under each of the two sets of responses (Performance and Expectations) and place the total score for each of the five columns in the blanks provided. Then add the column score total across from left to right for a total score for each set of ratings on each Best Practice. Graph your responses.

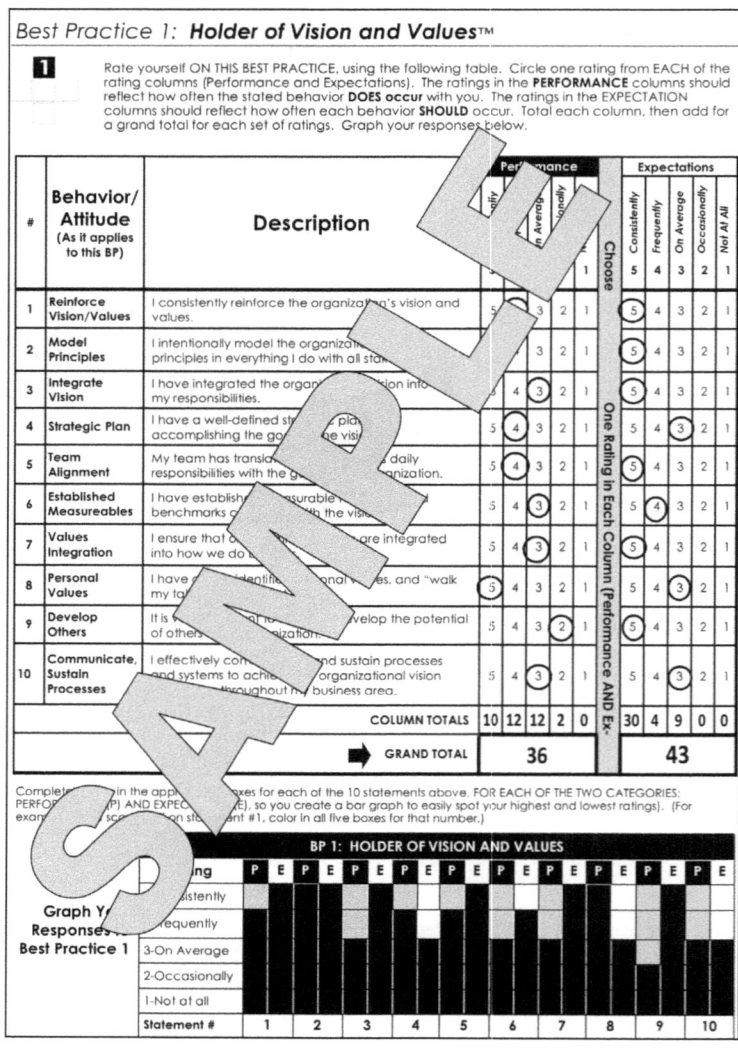

Best Practice 5: **Calibrator of Responsibility and Accountability**™

Rate yourself ON THIS BEST PRACTICE, using the following table. Circle one rating from EACH of the rating columns (Performance and Expectations). The ratings in the **PERFORMANCE** columns should reflect how often the stated behavior **DOES occur** with you. The ratings in the EXPECTATION columns should reflect how often each behavior **SHOULD** occur. Total each column, then add for a grand total for each set of ratings. Graph your responses below.

#	Behavior/Attitude (As it applies to this BP)	Description	Performance: Consistently 5	Frequently 4	On Average 3	Occasionally 2	Not At All 1		Expectations: Consistently 5	Frequently 4	On Average 3	Occasionally 2	Not At All 1
1	Strategic Plan with Checks and Balances	I execute the organization's strategic plan and use appropriate checks and balances to reach the goals.	5	4	3	2	1	Choose One Rating in Each Column (Performance AND Expectations)	5	4	3	2	1
2	Know Milestone Status	I have my "finger on the pulse" of the organization and know our milestone status.	5	4	3	2	1		5	4	3	2	1
3	Team Members Clear about Responsibilities	Individuals in my team are clear about position responsibilities and how they fit into the organization's direction and deliverables.	5	4	3	2	1		5	4	3	2	1
4	Require Peak Performance/	I require peak performance and support everyone with appropriate resources.	5	4	3	2	1		5	4	3	2	1
5	Feedback and Appropriate Action	I provide regular feedback and coaching, and take action when performance does not meet stated expectations.	5	4	3	2	1		5	4	3	2	1
6	Personal, Organizational	I have clearly defined accountabilities for myself and my organization.	5	4	3	2	1		5	4	3	2	1
7	Action Plan, Provision for Adjustments	I have a clearly developed action plan with benchmarks and milestones, and provisions for making adjustments along the way.	5	4	3	2	1		5	4	3	2	1
8	Urgency in Achievement	I model a sense of urgency both in getting things done and responding to change.	5	4	3	2	1		5	4	3	2	1
9	Alert to Trends, Recalibrates	I am alert to trends that potentially affect results, and re-calibrate action plans where necessary.	5	4	3	2	1		5	4	3	2	1
10	Team Commitment, Appropriate Consequences	I have gained commitment from everyone in my area of responsibility, and have established accountabilities with appropriate consequences and rewards.	5	4	3	2	1		5	4	3	2	1
		COLUMN TOTALS											
		➡ **GRAND TOTAL**											

Completely color in the appropriate boxes for each of the 10 statements above, FOR EACH OF THE TWO CATEGORIES: PERFORMANCE (P) AND EXPECTATION (E), so you create a bar graph to easily spot your highest and lowest ratings). (For example, if you scored "5" on statement #1, color in all five boxes for that number.)

Graph Your Responses to Best Practice 5

BP 5: CALIBRATOR OF RESPONSIBILITY AND ACCOUNTABILITY™																				
Rating	P	E	P	E	P	E	P	E	P	E	P	E	P	E	P	E	P	E	P	E
5-Consistently																				
4-Frequently																				
3-On Average																				
2-Occasionally																				
1-Not at all																				
Statement #	1		2		3		4		5		6		7		8		9		10	

APPLY THE BASICS

Critical Success Skills: Core Competencies

A calibrator consistently compares results against vision and values, and to established milestones and road maps. He or she provides a good and consistent example of accomplishing tasks and meeting shared goals, seeks to determine if actions measure up to standards and levels of excellence, and shows where learning is needed and new behaviors need to be developed. This leader keeps both internal and external focus, is ready and able to observe and respond to change and equips and congratulates everyone for responsible, professional efforts. This kind of calibration of responsibility and accountability is not about discipline, punishment, hall monitors, rule books or pointed fingers. It is a standard set by leadership by which the whole community has ownership of the process—and therefore is wholly accountable for progress made during that process. These critical success skills outline the behaviors that enable the leader to guide all individual parts of the community to contribute their very best to the process and share the results.

1. Execute the organization's strategic plan and use appropriate checks and balances to reach the goals.
2. Have your "finger on the pulse" of the organization and know your milestone status.
3. Be sure individuals on your team are clear about position responsibilities and how they fit into the organization's direction and deliverables.
4. Require peak performance and support everyone with appropriate resources.
5. Provide regular feedback and coaching, and take action when performance does not meet stated expectations.
6. Have clearly defined accountabilities for yourself and for your organization.
7. Have a clearly developed action plan with benchmarks and milestones, and provisions for making adjustments along the way.
8. Model a sense of urgency both in getting things done and responding to change.
9. Be alert to trends that potentially affect results, and re-calibrate action plans where necessary.
10. Gain commitment from everyone in your area of responsibility, and have established accountabilities with appropriate consequences and rewards.

Essence: *Being* a Legacy Leader
BE-Attitudes of a Calibrator of Responsibility and Accountability

We would expect the core being, the essence of a Calibrator of Responsibility and Accountability, to include such BE-attitudes as responsible, consistent, accountable, vision-grounded, and a problem solver to begin the list. As we have stated before, however, a *Legacy* Leader's BE-attitudes and aptitudes begin with a foundational core that all other attitudes and qualities will build upon or derive from. These core essentials are what allow the great leader to build leadership legacy, and apply learning to become true Calibrators of Responsibility and Accountability. We have listed the features we consider the Top Five BE-attitudes for your consideration in this Legacy Practice. These are not listed in any order of importance. Brief descriptions follow.

> ☐ **Results-Oriented**
> ☐ **An Analyst**
> ☐ **Vigilant/Committed**
> ☐ **Aware/Alert**
> ☐ **Answerable**

A Legacy Leader, a Calibrator of Responsibility and Accountability, IS:

1. **Results-Oriented**
2. **An Analyst**
3. **Vigilant/Committed**
4. **Aware/Alert**
5. **Answerable**

1. **Results-Oriented**
This person has a definite clarity of purpose and uses this clarity to drive behavior and performance to achieve results. These leaders have complete understanding of *why* they and others do *anything*, and always align their actions toward accomplishing goals and meeting vision. They never take their eye off desired results. There is very little to no "wasted motion" for these people. They tend to take advantage of every opportunity to produce results.

2. **An Analyst**
This person has the ability to analyze, diagnose and evaluate information, situations, issues or the environment around them. This is generally an inherent trait, but can be developed with focused practice. These people are usually able to "take in" details and information automatically in a way that allows them to constantly be aware of the real picture, wherever they are, whatever they are doing. They notice things that others may miss, and generally use the information to maintain a truthful picture of situations and conditions.

3. **Vigilant/Committed**
This person is constantly attentive and observant and able to "size up" things quickly. These people tend to be watchful at all times. This aptitude goes hand in hand with the one above, the ability to analyze. As the vigilant person takes in data, that data is analyzed automatically to yield accurate feedback on any situation at any time. Vigilant leaders are also committed to their vision and stated goals, and to their vigilance in keeping them.

4. Aware/Alert
This person has either an inherent or practiced awareness of the world around them. These leaders are able, at any given time, to provide an accurate and truthful portrait of their environments. They are not only aware of details and whole pictures, but are also alert to potential changes. They generally have internal "markers" set as guidelines for analysis and comparison. Again, this attitude is a refinement of the ones above. An analyst must be able to take the information in, be alert, aware and vigilant in this data gathering process, in order to accurately diagnose and evaluate.

5. Answerable
This person innately understands and practices responsibility and accountability. They hold themselves answerable to others to perform, and then liable to account for that performance. These leaders have complete awareness of the concept of action and reaction, behavior and consequences. They are guided by internal values and will model behavior that influences others to do the same. These people have no understanding of "ducking blame," don't engage in cover ups, and are completely open to scrutiny.

BE-ATTITUDE SELF ASSESSMENT
How developed is your core being for becoming a Legacy Leader in this Legacy Practice? After reading the descriptions of these BE-Attitudes above, rate yourself *(circle one)* on the following scale, then go on to the steps and questions that follow.

	BE-ATTITUDES of a Calibrator of Responsibility and Accountability	RATING: 5=all the time, 0=not at all
1	I results-oriented.	5 4 3 2 1 0
2	I am an "analyst."	5 4 3 2 1 0
3	I am vigilant and committed.	5 4 3 2 1 0
4	I am aware and alert.	5 4 3 2 1 0
5	I am answerable.	5 4 3 2 1 0

Where do your ratings fall? How many 5's? Any 2's or below? Any zeros? Here are some suggestions for building the core being of a Calibrator of Responsibility and Accountability.

1. **Choose your two highest ratings**. Determine how you can leverage these strengths to be even more effective in developing and living your leadership legacy. **Also choose two of your lowest** rating attitudes to be your "work on" areas for improvement. Use the questions below to build your BE-attitudes.

2. **Think of someone you know to be this**, to have this attitude, for each of the two areas you selected for improvement. For example, if you scored yourself low in being seamless in your behavior in all places, who do you know whose behavior *is* seamless (past or present)? Identify one person for each of the areas you want to develop and do the following exercises. Write the attitudes and person's name in the space provided:

   ATTITUDE   **PERSON I KNOW WHO DISPLAYS THIS ATTITUDE**
   1.
   2.

   Consider the following for each attitude, and person listed:

   a. What does this person do that lets me, and others, know he or she is _____ (BE-Attitude)?

   b. How can I emulate this behavior/attitude?

   c. How will this behavior help me become a better leader? A Legacy Leader?

3. After completing the above steps, **make a commitment** to improve. Choose one of your "work on" attitudes each week, and focus on improving that attitude in all you think, do and speak.
   a. Be aware of your behavior and thought processes during the week, as they pertain to that attitude.
   b. Create a mental reminder that will alert you to old behavior and thought patterns you want to change.
   c. When you are alerted to old behavior and thought patterns, change them immediately, if possible. If not, use that experience to help remind you in the future. Consider what triggered this old behavior or attitude, and how you can respond differently in the future.
   d. Evaluate your week for progress and determine how you can improve this attitude next week.
   e. The following week, add another "work on" attitude as your focus, but don't forget or neglect the first one.
   f. Keep doing this until you notice a definite change (improvement), so that your improved attitude has become part of you, part of your core being as a Legacy Leader. Chances are if *you* notice an improvement, others will as well.
   g. If journaling is familiar and comfortable for you, consider keeping track of your BE-Attitude development. Brush away discouragement if things don't change immediately. They will, especially if this is the way you want to be. Sometimes we just need to rethink or reframe how we think and do.

WRITE ANY COMMENTS BELOW YOU THINK MIGHT HELP YOU STRENGTHEN THESE BE-ATTITUDES...

NOTES

DRILL DOWNS
Best Practice 5

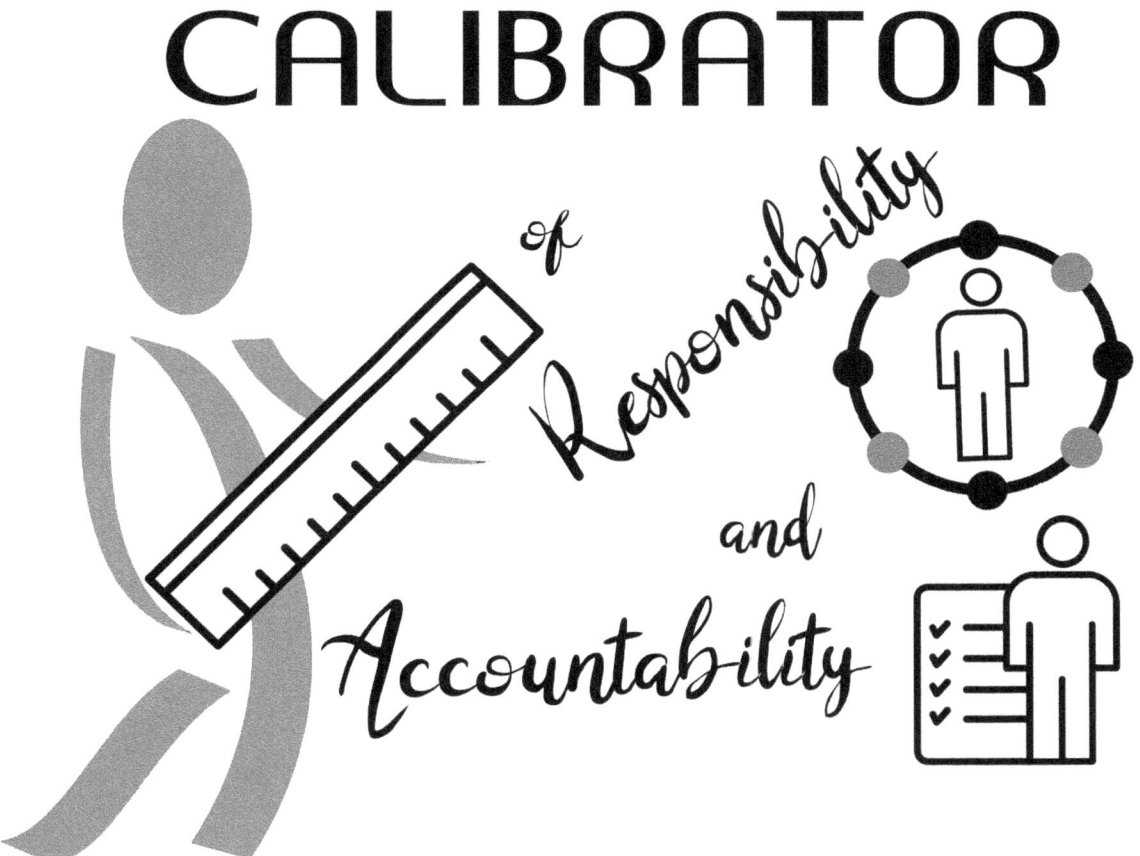

CALIBRATOR
of Responsibility and Accountability

The following section includes drill down *(more targeted and focused)* opportunities for each of the ten critical success skills for Best Practice 5. You may wish to complete the ones you have determined you need to strengthen first, but in order to truly round out your competencies and skills in this best practice, it is best to complete them all.

Drill Down 5:1

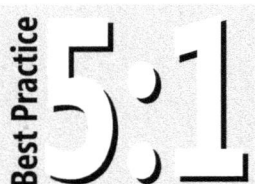

Best Practice 5:1

CRITICAL SUCCESS SKILL #1:
Execute the organization's strategic plan and use appropriate checks and balances to reach the goals.

Calibrator of Responsibility and Accountability™

Executing the Strategic Plan

BP1, Critical Success Skill #4 states: *"Have a well-defined strategic plan for accomplishing the goals of the vision."* BP1 is Holding Vision and Values. The worksheets in that Best Practice were designed to have you develop and refine a strategic plan, both for the organization as a whole, and for you as a leader in your area of responsibility. Best Practice 5 is where the "rubber meets the road," so to speak. It's about **DOING** (accomplishing) the vision, and **CHECKING** your progress.

- Reference the strategic plan you outlined in the Application Focus (BP1/CSS4) mentioned above. Have you been executing that plan? Is it working? How do you know? Indicate any changes you may have to make to your plan, and how you will refine your DOING of this plan.

Something to Think About...

"The vision must be followed by the venture. It is not enough to stare up the steps—we must step up the stairs."
Vance Havne

So, you have a vision. What's next? How do you follow it with the "venture?" To go up a flight of stairs, you can count each step one at a time and know exactly where you are. How will you know where you are in reaching the organizational vision? What about area vision, and yes, even personal vision?

ANSWERS

Using Appropriate Checks and Balances

"Checks and Balances" is a phrase we all know well as a tool to keep government functioning within certain guidelines. The same can be applied to an organization. The dictionary defines this as **"limits imposed on all [areas of an organization] by vesting in each [area] the right to amend or void those acts of another that fall within its purview."**

- How does this apply to you and your area of responsibility within your organization? Can you detail clearly your checks and balances, both within the organization, and within your area of responsibility?

- Accountability is an unpopular topic, whether within an organization, within a team, or personally. What thoughts do you have on a personal level about accountability? Are there any areas of your professional or personal life where accountability needs to be defined and reinforced? What can you do about those?

5:1 continued

TOP THREE

List your top 3 learnings, top 3 action plans, or top 3 personal reminders regarding this Critical Success Skill.

Drill Down 5:2

Best Practice 5:2

CRITICAL SUCCESS SKILL #2:
Have your "finger on the pulse" of the organization and know your milestone status.

Calibrator of Responsibility and Accountability™

Your "finger on the pulse"

How often do you take your own pulse? Probably not often, unless you are suffering from some medical ailment. We assume our hearts are beating normally most of the time. In business, this assumption can be fatal. Like taking a physical pulse, keeping your finger on the pulse of the organization, or the pulse of your area of responsibility, may seem to be awkward and time consuming. With practice, focus, and commitment this becomes second nature. **Consider this:**

Something to Think About...

"Financial outcomes alone will not tell you whether your organization is or will continue to be successful. There are other perspectives to consider...."
Brian Ward in "The New Accountability, Part 2" www.affinitymc.com

"Like a person who walks briskly into a room and forgets why, groups and organizations can lose sight of their purpose. So they run faster to make up for their lack of focus. By failing to take occasional detours from the daily grind of the long journey to refocus, reenergize, and rejuvenate, everyone becomes worn down and less effective. Leaders actively pay attention to the context and culture of their families, groups, or organization. They ensure that Vision, Values, and Purpose are alive and at the center of focus." *(from Growing the Distance: Timeless Principles for Personal, Career, and Family Success by Jim Clemmer, founder of the Clemmer Group)*

- How, and how often, do you consciously "take the pulse" of this organization, and your area of responsibility? Has it become so automatic that you always have your "finger on the pulse?" Do you know at any given time the "health" of your organization, or your team? If not, what can you do now in order to never lose that focus?

The comment above is taken from an article about the Balanced Scorecard, a relatively recent leadership and management tool to "get a grip on strategy, accountability and organizational alignment." What are the "other perspectives" that your organization needs to consider?

ANSWERS

Knowing "milestone" status

The beats of a heart are the milestone status for the health of the body. Every organization has different milestone markers, just like a map has milepost signs. You would not think to travel in an unfamiliar place without consulting a map and the milepost markers on the roads you travel.

- What are the significant events or points in the organization that serve as "milestones?"

- Loosely using the "Balanced Scorecard" approach of Financial, Customer, Internal and Learning Perspectives, how do organizational "milestones" fit into these categories of measurement? Do you know the status of each one? What perspectives provide a "Balanced Scorecard" for your organization?

5:2 continued

TOP THREE

List your top 3 learnings, top 3 action plans, or top 3 personal reminders regarding this Critical Success Skill.

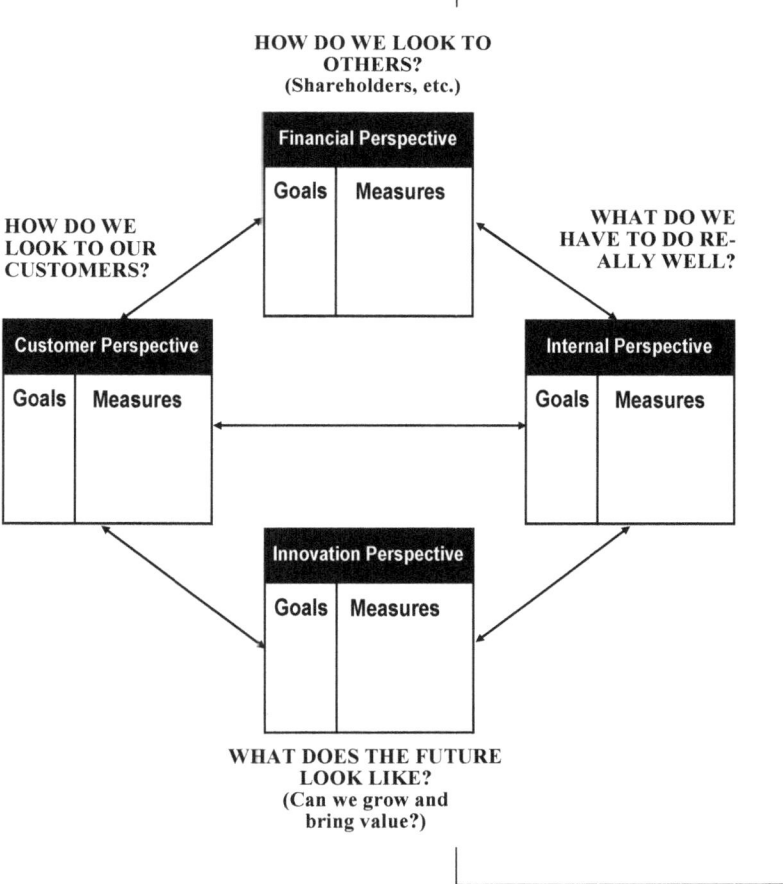

Drill Down 5:3

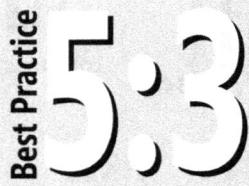

CRITICAL SUCCESS SKILL #3:
Ensure individuals on your team are clear about position responsibilities and how they fit into the organization's direction and deliverables.

Calibrator of Responsibility and Accountability™

Position Responsibilities

We all know about job descriptions and the importance of insuring that team members understand their individual and group responsibilities. The big questions are how and how often do you give conscious thought to this?

- How, and how often, do you communicate position responsibilities within your functional area? What can affect both your type and frequency of communication, and the responsibilities themselves?

Something to Think About...

"Throw out your tired old performance management systems that attempt to focus attention on the individual performer. We live in an interconnected world, where none of us are so detached that our personal contribution to organizational success can be reliably isolated and measured. Performance appraisal systems that focus on individual performance are notoriously ineffective at improving overall organizational performance."

Brian Ward in "The New Accountability, Part 2,"

To some, the above statement is downright blasphemous. What do you think? How might this have relevance in your area of responsibility?

- Making people clear about position responsibilities is not about giving orders. **"Arrogance of office leads to just giving orders, not gaining the respect and commitment of others, and erodes the strength and vitality of the organization, leaving only the weak and beaten."** *(Robert Dunham, former Vice President of Motorola Computer Systems).* If the communication and clarity of position responsibilities is not about giving orders, what IS it about? What are its components, and what does it look and sound like?

ANSWERS

Organizational "Fit"

A person's individual responsibilities are woven into the fabric of a team and the larger organization. Do your employees know their "fit?" Each person needs to be able to have a line of sight from their contributions to the organizational goals and vision. Consider these statements:

> **"Giving employees a sense of mission is important...Employees are typically much happier with their jobs when they understand how their work fits into the big picture."** *("The Right Stuff," Shari Caudron)*

> **"To sustain passion for a task, people have to feel that their work matters to the organization and they and their work are important."** *(T. Amabile in "How to Kill Creativity, Part 2," Harvard Business Review)* The knowledge of responsibility is not enough.

- What do you think about the comments above? Whose responsibility is it to make sure people know they matter to the organization's direction and deliverables? How does this relate to your area of responsibility, and what are you doing, or can you do, about it?

5:3
continued

TOP THREE

List your top 3 learnings, top 3 action plans, or top 3 personal reminders regarding this Critical Success Skill.

Drill Down 5:4

CRITICAL SUCCESS SKILL #4:
Require peak performance and support everyone with appropriate resources.

Calibrator of Responsibility and Accountability™

Requiring Peak Performance

This is easier said than done, isn't it? What is involved in this simple statement? Performance is more than meeting quotas or expectations. Performance involves knowing the employee and their capabilities, knowing the team dynamics and interrelationships, monitoring, accountability and honesty.

- Exactly HOW do you require peak performance? Be specific.

- How do you **communicate** your requirement for this?

Consider this: **"You have to be honest with people. You have to tell them the truth about their performance. You have to tell them face-to-face and you have to tell it to them over and over again. Holding frank, one-on-one conversations with every member of the organization is essential to success...Accentuate the positive at every possible opportunity and at the same time, emphasize the next goal that**

Something to Think About...

"You must not retain for one instant any man [or woman] in a responsible position where you have become doubtful of his ability to do his job. This matter calls for more courage than any other thing you will have to do, but I expect you to be perfectly cold-blooded about it."
Dwight D. Eisenhower

Ouch! This seems rather brutal on first reading, but what truth comes through here? If you are requiring peak performance, what do you do when requirements are not met? Do you agree with this statement? How does it affect your work?

ANSWERS

needs to be fulfilled..." *(B. Parcells, "The Tough Work of Turning Around a Team," Harvard Business Review)*

- Are you honest about requiring peak performance, or are you tempted to "let things slide?" How can you require peak performance without turning your area of responsibility into a corporate boot camp?

Supporting with Appropriate Resources

Every employee must be provided with the right tools to do his or her job. These tools can include everything from material goods to specialized implements, information and timelines, training and development. Beyond this, however, there is another resource often overlooked: personal support. Support touches in the area of Best Practice 3, but is also addressed here as an "appropriate" resource. **"Leaders must show concern for the development of employees and provide support and coaching."** *("The Right Stuff," Shari Caudron)*

- Exactly what are the "appropriate resources" for your team members? Make a list and consider everything necessary in order for them to fulfill their responsibilities. Ask each person what they need to do his or her job. Are you providing all these things in adequate measure?

- Beyond the resources you indicated above, what personal support for your team members is also needed to ensure their success in current positions, and their continued success and development? How do you mentor them for success?

5:4 continued

TOP THREE

List your top 3 learnings, top 3 action plans, or top 3 personal reminders regarding this Critical Success Skill.

Drill Down 5:5

CRITICAL SUCCESS SKILL #5:
Provide regular feedback and coaching, and take action when performance does not meet stated expectations.

Calibrator of Responsibility and Accountability™

Something to Think About...

"Teach a highly educated person that it is not a disgrace to fail and that he must analyze every failure to find its cause. He [or she] must learn how to fail intelligently, for failing is one of the greatest arts in the world."
— Charles F. Kettering

We don't like to use that word—FAILURE. But nothing is accomplished when we don't honestly own up to it. How can failures become springboards to success? How can we do this "intelligently?" How can you help others do this?

Feedback and Coaching

To provide successful feedback and coaching, it is important to fully understand these terms. Feedback in itself is merely information about performance. This can be good or bad. Feedback with coaching, however, is what makes the information constructive, useful and dynamic. One of the simplest definitions of coaching is by Dennis Kinlaw: **"Successful coaching is a mutual conversation that follows a predictable process and leads to superior performance, commitment to sustained improvement and positive relationships."** Coaching is encouragement with accountability for success. It is not sugar-coating, avoidance or denial, OR hype. The coach speaks the truth with a positive plan.

- Do you provide regular feedback AND coaching for those in your area of responsibility? How? How would you describe your style in this? Have you acted as coach when giving feedback? How do people respond? Describe your current style, and how you could improve in this area.

ANSWERS

Taking Action when Performance Falls Short

5:5 continued

TOP THREE

List your top 3 learnings, top 3 action plans, or top 3 personal reminders regarding this Critical Success Skill.

This action goes hand in hand with the previous success skill. You might require peak performance, but eventually and undoubtedly there will be those times when someone doesn't perform at the level required. Now what? What actions do you take?

- Describe your typical action steps when confronted with performance that does not meet stated standards. Consider your personal performance in these times, and that of others, either individually or corporately. What is your attitude? How do you coach through these times? If you do not already have an action plan, carefully consider the potential steps to turn failures into successes.

- Consider this: **"Leadership has less to do with position than it has with disposition."** *(John C. Maxwell)* How does this apply to the above action plan for less than acceptable performance?

Drill Down 5:6

CRITICAL SUCCESS SKILL #6:
Have clearly defined accountabilities for yourself and for your organization.

Calibrator of Responsibility and Accountability™

Defined Personal Accountabilities

Having clearly defined accountabilities means first knowing the vision and the goals, then knowing what it takes to satisfy them, and finally and most importantly for this Best Practice, how you are accountable for them.

Personal accountabilities are those goals and vision which you have determined as desirable for YOU personally, outside those of the organization. Personal accountabilities involve knowing who you are. Consider this: **"Know Thyself...another important factor in becoming a good leader is self-awareness. In other words, the ability to understand yourself so well that you not only know how you would behave in a given situation, but you understand the impact your actions have on others."** *(from "The Right Stuff" by S. Caudron)*

- Do you have personal accountabilities? What are they, and how do you hold yourself accountable for them? Do your personal accountabilities show self-awareness?

Something to Think About...

"Don't measure yourself by what you have accomplished, but what you should have accomplished with your ability."

John Wooden

Too often we are satisfied if we merely meet stated expectations, even if they fall below our abilities. Is our accountability only to what others expect? What about what we should expect of ourselves, knowing our abilities? Do you agree with the statement above? What would this mean to you and your team? What would you have to know first? What would be the result?

ANSWERS

Defined Organizational Accountabilities

5:6
continued

TOP THREE

List your top 3 learnings, top 3 action plans, or top 3 personal reminders regarding this Critical Success Skill.

We assume here that you are well aware of your organization's vision and goals. We also assume that you know what it takes to successfully achieve them. But having clearly defined organizational accountabilities involves another two-fold step—knowing how **you** are accountable for them, and then BEING accountable.

- Do you know fully WHAT you are accountable FOR? Who are you accountable TO? Explain.

- Do you **OWN** your accountability? Consider this: "**Accept responsibility for your piece of the mess. If you have been in a senior role for awhile and there's a problem, it is almost certain that you had some part in creating it and are part of the reason it has not yet been addressed. Even if you are new, or outside the organization, you need to identify those behaviors you practice or values you embody that could stifle the very change you want to advance.**" (*Ronald Heifetz and Marty Linsk in "Managing People Politics" CIO Magazine*) Do you accept appropriate responsibility and accountability for your functional area? Explain.

Drill Down 5:7

CRITICAL SUCCESS SKILL #7:
Have a clearly developed action plan with benchmarks and milestones, and provisions for making adjustments along the way.

Calibrator of Responsibility and Accountability™

Something to Think About...

"Failures don't plan to fail; they fail to plan."

Harvey Mackay

Simple, but true. Your strategic plan must include every facet of reaching your vision, including planning for and executing course corrections. Being a Calibrator of Responsibility and Accountability is at the heart of planning for re-alignment and adjustments to the strategic plan. How is being a Calibrator foundational to success? How do you do this in your area of responsibility?

Calibrating Action Plans with Markers and Milestones

Perhaps the best analogy of an action plan is a road map. You have marked your starting point (where you are now) and your final destination (where you want to be). The "benchmarks" and "milestones" are equivalent to the mile markers you pass, indicating you are still on the right road (or not). We have discussed and given you opportunity in these Application Focus sheets for the development of a strategic plan. In Drill Down BP1-CSS6, you were asked to list five different Key Performance Indicators (KPIs) that serve as your mile markers. The roadmap is in place. The big question is, now that you have begun the "trip" how do you make course corrections?

- What plan do you have in place to make corrections and adjustments if you have discovered that you are not in alignment with your stated KPIs?

- How aware are you of course and direction? How frequently do you check the mile markers? How will you know when you need to make adjustments?

ANSWERS

- How will you implement alignments back to stated strategy?

- How will you lead your team to follow and make their own adjustments?

- Can you think of a specific example where you have successfully adjusted your action plan based on your KPIs? Describe.

Consider this: **"Characteristics of the OLD Accountability included Fixed goals, fixed plans, little flexibility, [and] assume that the world is in a fixed state and can be 'managed.' The NEW Accountability has planning in real time, includes all members of the collaborative network and assumes that the world is in a constant state of flux, yet can be understood and worked with."** *(From "The New Accountability" by Brian Ward)*

- How does this statement affect your action plan, your benchmarks and milestones, and your adjustments? Should you make any changes?

5:7 continued

TOP THREE

List your top 3 learnings, top 3 action plans, or top 3 personal reminders regarding this Critical Success Skill.

Drill Down 5:8

CRITICAL SUCCESS SKILL #8:
Model a sense of urgency both in getting things done and responding to change.

Calibrator of Responsibility and Accountability™

Modeling Urgency in Accomplishment

Going back to your roadmap, you have most likely established some time restraints for the trip you intend to take. Modeling urgency for the journey is about setting the pace for a timely trip, "making good time" as we sometimes say while traveling from one place to another. Modeling urgency is not about **not** stopping when you need to, but about leading your traveling companions in a steady pursuit of your goals, as measured against your time commitments.

- How, exactly, do you model urgency for your team members? How do you do this without forfeiting needed pauses, and without creating a "frantic" environment?

- Define your "sense of urgency" in getting things done, and meeting the organization's vision and goals. What is this to you?

Something to Think About...

"...management is about coping with complexity... leadership is all about coping with change. In recent years, with factors like the pace of technological evolution, globalization, deregulation and shifting demographics, major change is required more and more quickly to not just cope, but to survive and compete effectively."

John P. Kotter in "What Leaders Really Do" Harvard Business Review

How does a sense of urgency in responding to change further define managers and leaders? Why is this important for your work?

★ ANSWERS

Consider this: **"The one facet that can make or break a leader is in knowing when to make critical decisions and when not to. All [else] must be viewed as subservient to getting the timing of critical decisions right....get the timing wrong on critical decisions and everything else stands to be nullified. Great leaders move with appropriate speed. They don't believe everything must be done immediately...they know how to prioritize, and how to get their team to prioritize. As well, they engage in timely follow-through to ensure actions that are committed to happen in a well coordinated and timely way."** *(from "The Five Key Facets of Quality Leadership" by Brian Ward)*

- How do you measure up in modeling urgency as it relates to this statement? Explain.

5:8 continued

TOP THREE

List your top 3 learnings, top 3 action plans, or top 3 personal reminders regarding this Critical Success Skill.

Responding to Change

Knowing **"when to hold them and when to fold them"** is one thing. Responding with a sense of urgency is quite another. We've heard the saying "you snooze, you lose." Some say that for leaders, this must be a "sixth" sense.

- What do you think? How aware are you of the need for change and urgency involved in making those changes? What cautions should be applied here? How well do you respond to change, AND to the need for change? How do you help your team members do this?

- How do you teach others to be flexible and agile in their response to change and chaos?

Drill Down 5:9

Best Practice 5:9

CRITICAL SUCCESS SKILL #9:
Be alert to trends that potentially affect results, and re-calibrate action plans where necessary.

Calibrator of Responsibility and Accountability™

Being Alert to Trends

In an earlier Focus we discussed the importance of having your "finger on the pulse" of your organization at all times. This alone is not enough, however. You must also have your finger on the pulse of the world at large—your competition, technology, global trends, politics, economics and just about every other indicator of trends that may affect your business results.

- How alert are you to trends that potentially affect results? What tools do you utilize to do this? What is your priority and attitude about this?

- What trends, in particular, are of primary interest to you in your area of responsibility?

Something to Think About...

"Effective CEOs have a strong external focus and get stimulated by details of what's happening in their markets, details others might find boring. A CEO has to do what must be done, what reality demands, not what he [necessarily] wants to do."

R. Charan and C. Geoffrey in "Why CEOs Fail" Fortune

Maybe you are not the CEO now, but one day.... Do you have the "right stuff?" You are the CEO, effectively, of your area of responsibility. Can you relate to the above statement? How does it apply to your work?

ANSWERS

- Consider this: **"Keep your mind open to change at all times. Welcome it. Court it. It is only by examining and re-examining your opinions and ideas that you can progress."** *(Dale Carnegie)* How do trends relate to change? Are you open to them, and do you welcome change like the statement above suggests we should? Is your leadership more like an ostrich or an eagle?

5:9 continued

TOP THREE

List your top 3 learnings, top 3 action plans, or top 3 personal reminders regarding this Critical Success Skill.

Re-calibrating Action Plans

In the article titled "New Leaders, New Agenda" by Alison Overholt in Fast Company, Alfred Chuang, then CEO of BEA Systems, Inc. stated: **"The events of September 11 and the recession have affected BEA on many levels…my job as BEA's CEO is to recalibrate the madness into reality."** *The article went on to state that Chuang "trimmed costs and increased communication with employees. He institutionalized company Webcast, and has managers walk around the office more often talking to people about their careers."* This is an example of RE-active re-calibration. Sometimes trends or changes force us into re-calibration, desired or not.

- Describe how you can be PRO-active in your re-calibration of action plans for your area of responsibility, as you are aware and alert to trends that may affect your results.

Drill Down 5:10

Best Practice 5:10

CRITICAL SUCCESS SKILL #10:
Gain commitment from everyone in your area of responsibility, and have established accountabilities with appropriate consequences and rewards.

Calibrator of Responsibility and Accountability™

Gaining Commitment

Without followers, there are no leaders. Consider this: **"A necessary requirement for a leader is to gain confidence from the people he [or she] works with, otherwise there will be no followers, and to gain confidence in a leader, the followers must be convinced that he [or she] has integrity, speaks the truth and has authority. Be it absolute or delegated."** *(Francisco Magalhaes in "Leaders and Followers")*

- Commitment stems from confidence in leadership. Have you gained commitment from everyone in your area of responsibility? How do you know? How is it demonstrated? How was it earned?

- Are your team members convinced of your integrity? Do they know you speak the truth, and have authority? How? Do you make a conscious call for commitment? How?

Something to Think About...

"Celebrate: Achieving goals and surpassing milestones deserve credit. Celebrating these accomplishments underscores the value that each person brings to the table and confirms expected behaviors—all while serving as motivators for future learning."

Ivy Sea
"Valuing People" Series: "Six Coaching Strategies You Can Apply in the Workplace"

ANSWERS

How do you appropriately celebrate accomplishments with your team? Why is this important?

- What does this quote say to you, especially in your leadership role? **"Ownership and excellence do not come from order takers, and usually ordering produces resentful avoidance, when what we really want is the ownership, pride, and passion that comes when people commit to what they are doing."** *(From "Top 14 Mistakes Senior Managers Make" by Robert Dunham)*

Accountabilities, Consequences and Rewards

We have previously discussed performance and accountabilities. We have hinted at consequences, but said little so far about rewards. We can hold people accountable, but unless there are appropriate consequences and rewards, accountability has little meaning. Like everything else in leadership, a good plan for these things can make all the difference in the world.

- Do you have a plan for consequences and rewards? Have you given this ample thought before you need to implement either of these accountability factors? Do your team members know them? Are they committed to their follow-through?

5:10 continued

TOP THREE

List your top 3 learnings, top 3 action plans, or top 3 personal reminders regarding this Critical Success Skill.

Legacy Leadership Application Workbook

Mapping the Plan for Organizational Results

1 Use this template for developing a case for change (e.g., justifying budget items, developing action plans, or identifying measurements and milestones).

2 LEADER SHIFTS		**3** Observable and Measurable **DIFFERENCES** (What will you see)
FROM ➡	**TO**	
Identify language that clearly represents the current state and desired state (before and after shift).		When you reach the desired state, what changes will you be able to observe and measure?

ACTION ITEMS (Making it happen)	**7** RESULTS (Impact on the Organization)
4 How will you bring about the desired state? **HOW?**	In what ways will the organization be impacted (e.g. increased earnings per share, improved retention rates)?
5 Who possesses the appropriate strengths for this effort? **WHO WILL DO IT?**	
6 When do you expect completion? **PROJECTED TIMELINE**	

© 2017-2021. CoachWorks® International, Inc. Dallas, TX. All International Rights Reserved. Do not duplicate.

Legacy Leadership Application Workbook

Mapping the Plan for Professional Results

[1] Use this template to formulate a simple development plan for YOUR change

[2] LEADER SHIFTS		**[3] Observable and Measurable DIFFERENCES** (What will you see)
FROM ➡	**TO**	
List the top 5 areas you want to work on now in the FROM column in language that states your current behavior. List these behaviors again in the TO column to show the shift you will make. These are goal statements.		When you reach the desired state, what changes will you (and others) be able to observe and measure in these 5 areas?

ACTION ITEMS (Making it happen)	**[7] RESULTS** (Impact on you and others)
[4] How will you bring about the desired shift and growth?	What do you see as the impact of making these changes? On yourself? On others? On your business? On your organization?
[5] What resources do you need for this plan to succeed?	
[6] When do you expect to achieve your goals?	

Best Practice 5
Calibrator of Responsibility and Accountability™

Best Practice 5 Application Notes

Best Practice 5

Calibrator of Responsibility and Accountability™

Best Practice 5 Application Notes

Further Development

Important Questions

If I were making a "to do" list for my personal leadership development as a Legacy Leader®, what are my **top three** commitments to myself?

1.

2.

3.

With whom will I share my Action/Development Plan and when?

How will I know when I am a Legacy Leader®? What will success look like?

If the fundamental premise of a Legacy Leader® is to teach others to be Legacy Leaders®, then: What opportunities are available to me right now to teach LL to others?

What LL supporting materials, resources and techniques will I use to grow other leaders?

Which leaders in my organization/practice/workplace/other will I grow as Legacy Leaders® in the next four months? Year? Beyond?

What do I plan to do next in my professional development as a Legacy Leader?

Competency Inventory

Using the Inventory

This competency inventory is an opportunity for leaders to receive information about their level of competency in each of the five practice contexts of Legacy Leadership. It provides a direction for learning, a guide for leader development and a model for developing leadership fully.

Instructions for Completion

For each Best Practice there is a set of ten descriptive statements. YOU ARE ASKED TO PROVIDE A RATING FOR **TWO QUESTIONS** FOR EACH STATEMENT:

PERFORMANCE: How often **do I exhibit** this stated behavior/attitude?
EXPECTATIONS: How often is this stated behavior/attitude **expected to occur** in my position?

Read each statement carefully, and honestly rate yourself on a scale of 1 to 5 as follows:
This statement describes my behavior/attitude (PERFORMANCE COLUMN):
The statement describes how often this behavior/attitude should occur (EXPECTATIONS):

      1—Not At All
      2—Occasionally
      3—On Average
      4—Frequently
      5—Consistently

Rate yourself for BOTH Performance and Expectations using this scale. Answer all ten questions in each Best Practice, for a total of 50 questions, two responses (ratings) each question.

After you have rated each statement, total each column under each of the two sets of responses (Performance and Expectations) and place the added score for each of the five columns in the blanks provided. Then add the column score total across from left to right for a total score for each set of ratings on each Best Practice. Graph your responses on each page. ***See the sample page following.***

Complete the Master Scoring Grid on page 13.

Next Steps: Legacy Leader® Development Plan

After you have established your baseline as a starting point, you will be able to design a leader development plan including those areas you wish to upgrade your level of performance. See page 14 for a suggested format for your plan. Work with your coach and/or leader to carry out the plan and leverage the results.

Legacy Leadership Application Workbook

Best Practice 1: *Holder of Vision and Values*™

Rate yourself ON THIS BEST PRACTICE, using the following table. Circle one rating from EACH of the rating columns (Performance and Expectations). The ratings in the **PERFORMANCE** columns should reflect how often the stated behavior **DOES occur** with you. The ratings in the EXPECTATION columns should reflect how often each behavior **SHOULD** occur. Total each column, then add for a grand total for each set of ratings. Graph your responses below.

#	Behavior/Attitude (As it applies to this BP)	Description	Performance: Consistently 5	Frequently 4	On Average 3	Occasionally 2	Not At All 1	Choose One Rating in Each Column (Performance AND Ex-	Expectations: Consistently 5	Frequently 4	On Average 3	Occasionally 2	Not At All 1
1	Reinforce Vision/Values	I consistently reinforce the organization's vision and values.	5	④	3	2	1		⑤	4	3	2	1
2	Model Principles	I intentionally model the organization's principles in everything I do with all staff.	5	④	3	2	1		⑤	4	3	2	1
3	Integrate Vision	I have integrated the organization's vision into my responsibilities.	5	4	③	2	1		⑤	4	3	2	1
4	Strategic Plan	I have a well-defined strategic plan for accomplishing the goals of the vision.	5	④	3	2	1		5	4	③	2	1
5	Team Alignment	My team has translated their daily responsibilities with the goals of the organization.	5	④	3	2	1		⑤	4	3	2	1
6	Established Measureables	I have established measurable and benchmarks aligned with the vision.	5	4	③	2	1		5	④	3	2	1
7	Values Integration	I ensure that our values are integrated into how we do business.	5	4	③	2	1		⑤	4	3	2	1
8	Personal Values	I have clearly identified personal values, and "walk my talk".	⑤	4	3	2	1		5	4	③	2	1
9	Develop Others	It is important to develop the potential of others in the organization.	5	4	3	②	1		⑤	4	3	2	1
10	Communicate, Sustain Processes	I effectively communicate and sustain processes and systems to achieve the organizational vision throughout my business area.	5	4	③	2	1		5	4	③	2	1
		COLUMN TOTALS	10	12	12	2	0		30	4	9	0	0
		➡ **GRAND TOTAL**			36						43		

Complete (fill in) the appropriate boxes for each of the 10 statements above, FOR EACH OF THE TWO CATEGORIES: PERFORMANCE (P) AND EXPECTATIONS (E), so you create a bar graph to easily spot your highest and lowest ratings). (For example, if you scored a 5 on statement #1, color in all five boxes for that number.)

Graph Your Responses Best Practice 1

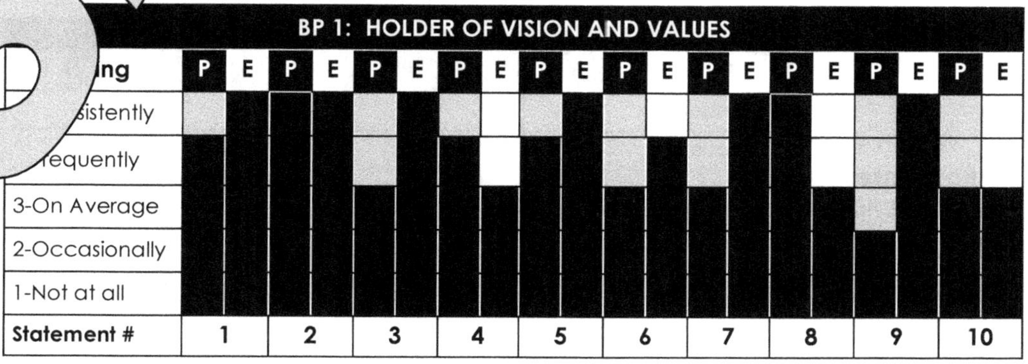

BP 1: HOLDER OF VISION AND VALUES

Rating	P	E	P	E	P	E	P	E	P	E	P	E	P	E	P	E	P	E	P	E
5-Consistently																				
4-Frequently																				
3-On Average																				
2-Occasionally																				
1-Not at all																				
Statement #	1		2		3		4		5		6		7		8		9		10	

© 2017-2021. CoachWorks® International, Inc. Dallas, TX. All International Rights Reserved. Do not duplicate.

Best Practice 1: **Holder of Vision and Values**™

Rate yourself ON THIS BEST PRACTICE, using the following table. Circle one rating from EACH of the rating columns (Performance and Expectations). The ratings in the **PERFORMANCE** columns should reflect how often the stated behavior **DOES occur** with you. The ratings in the EXPECTATION columns should reflect how often each behavior **SHOULD** occur. Total each column, then add for a grand total for each set of ratings. Graph your responses below.

#	Behavior/Attitude (As it applies to this BP)	Description	Performance						Expectations					
			Consistently 5	Frequently 4	On Average 3	Occasionally 2	Not At All 1		Consistently 5	Frequently 4	On Average 3	Occasionally 2	Not At All 1
1	Reinforce Vision/Values	I consistently reinforce the organization's vision and values.	5	4	3	2	1	Choose One Rating in Each Column (Performance AND Expectations)	5	4	3	2	1
2	Model Principles	I intentionally model the organization's guiding principles in everything I do with all stakeholders.	5	4	3	2	1		5	4	3	2	1
3	Integrate Vision	I have integrated the organization's vision into all of my responsibilities.	5	4	3	2	1		5	4	3	2	1
4	Strategic Plan	I have a well-defined strategic plan for accomplishing the goals of the vision.	5	4	3	2	1		5	4	3	2	1
5	Team Alignment	My team has translated and aligned its daily responsibilities with the goals of the organization.	5	4	3	2	1		5	4	3	2	1
6	Established Measureables	I have established measurable milestones and benchmarks congruent with the vision.	5	4	3	2	1		5	4	3	2	1
7	Values Integration	I ensure that organizational values are integrated into how we do business.	5	4	3	2	1		5	4	3	2	1
8	Personal Values	I have clearly identified personal values, and "walk my talk" in everything I do.	5	4	3	2	1		5	4	3	2	1
9	Develop Others	It is very important to me that I develop the potential of others in the organization.	5	4	3	2	1		5	4	3	2	1
10	Communicate, Sustain Processes	I effectively communicate and sustain processes and systems to achieve the organizational vision and values throughout my business area.	5	4	3	2	1		5	4	3	2	1
		COLUMN TOTALS											
		➡ **GRAND TOTAL**											

Completely color in the appropriate boxes for each of the 10 statements above, FOR EACH OF THE TWO CATEGORIES: PERFORMANCE (P) AND EXPECTATION (E), so you create a bar graph to easily spot your highest and lowest ratings). (For example, if you scored "5" on statement #1, color in all five boxes for that number.)

Graph Your Responses to Best Practice 1

BP 1: HOLDER OF VISION AND VALUES™																					
Rating	P	E	P	E	P	E	P	E	P	E	P	E	P	E	P	E	P	E	P	E
5-Consistently																				
4-Frequently																				
3-On Average																				
2-Occasionally																				
1-Not at all																				
Statement #	1		2		3		4		5		6		7		8		9		10	

Best Practice 2: Creator of Collaboration and Innovation™

Rate yourself ON THIS BEST PRACTICE, using the following table. Circle one rating from EACH of the rating columns (Performance and Expectations). The ratings in the **PERFORMANCE** columns should reflect how often the stated behavior **DOES occur** with you. The ratings in the EXPECTATION columns should reflect how often each behavior **SHOULD** occur. Total each column, then add for a grand total for each set of ratings. Graph your responses below.

#	Behavior/ Attitude (As it applies to this BP)	Description	Performance Consistently 5	Frequently 4	On Average 3	Occasionally 2	Not At All 1	Choose One Rating in Each Column (Performance AND Expectations)	Expectations Consistently 5	Frequently 4	On Average 3	Occasionally 2	Not At All 1
1	Innovative Possibilities	I create possibilities that are both innovative and sound for the organization.	5	4	3	2	1		5	4	3	2	1
2	Trusting Environment	I foster a learning, trusting environment where true collaboration and innovation are unleashed.	5	4	3	2	1		5	4	3	2	1
3	Masterful Listener	I am a masterful listener for both what is said and what is not said.	5	4	3	2	1		5	4	3	2	1
4	Comfortable Learning from	I am comfortable not knowing "the answers" and learning from individual perspectives.	5	4	3	2	1		5	4	3	2	1
5	Opportunities in Disagreement	I draw out differing perspectives and believe that disagreement is a learning opportunity.	5	4	3	2	1		5	4	3	2	1
6	Timely Questioning	I keep in mind the bigger picture while asking timely, tough questions.	5	4	3	2	1		5	4	3	2	1
7	Innovate for Future	I set the tone for thinking beyond where we are presently in order to innovate now for the future.	5	4	3	2	1		5	4	3	2	1
8	Organizational, Marketplace Projection	I can project how ideas may play out in the organization and marketplace.	5	4	3	2	1		5	4	3	2	1
9	Discern need (or not) for Change	I can discern, and assist others to understand, when change needs to occur and when it does not.	5	4	3	2	1		5	4	3	2	1
10	Facilitate Best Group Thinking	I am a masterful facilitator of conversations such that everyone contributes their best thinking toward the task/issue at hand.	5	4	3	2	1		5	4	3	2	1
		COLUMN TOTALS											
		➡ **GRAND TOTAL**											

Completely color in the appropriate boxes for each of the 10 statements above, FOR EACH OF THE TWO CATEGORIES: PERFORMANCE (P) AND EXPECTATION (E), so you create a bar graph to easily spot your highest and lowest ratings). (For example, if you scored "5" on statement #1, color in all five boxes for that number.)

Graph Your Responses to Best Practice 2

BP 2: CREATOR OF COLLABORATION AND INNOVATION™																				
Rating	P	E	P	E	P	E	P	E	P	E	P	E	P	E	P	E	P	E	P	E
5-Consistently																				
4-Frequently																				
3-On Average																				
2-Occasionally																				
1-Not at all																				
Statement #	1		2		3		4		5		6		7		8		9		10	

Best Practice 3: *Influencer of Inspiration and Leadership*™

Rate yourself ON THIS BEST PRACTICE, using the following table. Circle one rating from EACH of the rating columns (Performance and Expectations). The ratings in the **PERFORMANCE** columns should reflect how often the stated behavior **DOES occur** with you. The ratings in the EXPECTATION columns should reflect how often each behavior **SHOULD** occur. Total each column, then add for a grand total for each set of ratings. Graph your responses below.

#	Behavior/Attitude (As it applies to this BP)	Description	Performance: Consistently 5	Frequently 4	On Average 3	Occasionally 2	Not At All 1		Expectations: Consistently 5	Frequently 4	On Average 3	Occasionally 2	Not At All 1
1	Develop Relationships	I am very adept at developing and maintaining relationships.	5	4	3	2	1	Choose One Rating in Each Column (Performance AND Expectations)	5	4	3	2	1
2	Energy to Influence	I use my emotional intelligence and positive energy to influence others.	5	4	3	2	1		5	4	3	2	1
3	Model Positive Perspective	I choose to model the positive perspective in all situations.	5	4	3	2	1		5	4	3	2	1
4	Evoke Best in Others	I bring out the best in people.	5	4	3	2	1		5	4	3	2	1
5	Acknowledge Contributions	I constantly acknowledge and recognize the attributes and contributions of others.	5	4	3	2	1		5	4	3	2	1
6	Delegate for Development	I intentionally delegate for the development of others.	5	4	3	2	1		5	4	3	2	1
7	Showcase Others	I lead with a constant focus on showcasing others rather than myself.	5	4	3	2	1		5	4	3	2	1
8	Inspiring Risk Taker	I have the ability and courage to take risks and inspire others to follow.	5	4	3	2	1		5	4	3	2	1
9	Minimize Negative	I am able to make tough decisions that have minimal negative impact.	5	4	3	2	1		5	4	3	2	1
10	Meet goals thru Others/Humility, Resolve	I lead with humility and fierce resolve to accomplish the goals of the organization through others.	5	4	3	2	1		5	4	3	2	1
		COLUMN TOTALS											
		➡ **GRAND TOTAL**											

Completely color in the appropriate boxes for each of the 10 statements above, FOR EACH OF THE TWO CATEGORIES: PERFORMANCE (P) AND EXPECTATION (E), so you create a bar graph to easily spot your highest and lowest ratings). (For example, if you scored "5" on statement #1, color in all five boxes for that number.)

Graph Your Responses to Best Practice 3

BP 3: INFLUENCER OF INSPIRATION AND LEADERSHIP™																				
Rating	P	E	P	E	P	E	P	E	P	E	P	E	P	E	P	E	P	E	P	E
5-Consistently																				
4-Frequently																				
3-On Average																				
2-Occasionally																				
1-Not at all																				
Statement #	1		2		3		4		5		6		7		8		9		10	

Best Practice 4: **Advocator of Differences and Community**™

Rate yourself ON THIS BEST PRACTICE, using the following table. Circle one rating from EACH of the rating columns (Performance and Expectations). The ratings in the **PERFORMANCE** columns should reflect how often the stated behavior **DOES occur** with you. The ratings in the EXPECTATION columns should reflect how often each behavior **SHOULD** occur. Total each column, then add for a grand total for each set of ratings. Graph your responses below.

#	Behavior/ Attitude (As it applies to this BP)	Description	Performance Consistently 5	Frequently 4	On Average 3	Occasionally 2	Not At All 1		Expectations Consistently 5	Frequently 4	On Average 3	Occasionally 2	Not At All 1
1	Ready Advocate	I am able to take a stand for a person, practice, or cause.	5	4	3	2	1		5	4	3	2	1
2	Mentor for Visibility	I constantly raise the visibility of individuals by mentoring and developing them.	5	4	3	2	1	Choose One Rating in Each Column (Performance AND Expectations)	5	4	3	2	1
3	Strengths-Based Culture	I am an advocate for a strengths-based culture where everyone works from their strengths.	5	4	3	2	1		5	4	3	2	1
4	Connoisseur of Talent	I am a connoisseur of talent, recognizing, valuing and utilizing the best each person has to offer.	5	4	3	2	1		5	4	3	2	1
5	Team Diversity	I insist on having teams of individuals with diverse approaches and capabilities.	5	4	3	2	1		5	4	3	2	1
6	Cross-Functional Opportunities	I look for cross-functional opportunities where unique talent can be developed.	5	4	3	2	1		5	4	3	2	1
7	Inter-Department Collaboration	I promote inter-departmental collaboration rather than "silo" orientation.	5	4	3	2	1		5	4	3	2	1
8	Consider Greater Community	I consider the impact of actions on the greater community beyond organizational boundaries.	5	4	3	2	1		5	4	3	2	1
9	Internal-External Communication	I have ongoing dialogue and involvement with internal and external communities.	5	4	3	2	1		5	4	3	2	1
10	United Inclusive Environment	I promote an inclusive environment that unites towards a common focus.	5	4	3	2	1		5	4	3	2	1
		COLUMN TOTALS											
		➤ **GRAND TOTAL**											

Completely color in the appropriate boxes for each of the 10 statements above, FOR EACH OF THE TWO CATEGORIES: PERFORMANCE (P) AND EXPECTATION (E), so you create a bar graph to easily spot your highest and lowest ratings). (For example, if you scored "5" on statement #1, color in all five boxes for that number.)

Graph Your Responses to Best Practice 4

BP 4: ADVOCATOR OF DIFFERENCES AND COMMUNITY™																				
Rating	P	E	P	E	P	E	P	E	P	E	P	E	P	E	P	E	P	E	P	E
5-Consistently																				
4-Frequently																				
3-On Average																				
2-Occasionally																				
1-Not at all																				
Statement #	1		2		3		4		5		6		7		8		9		10	

Best Practice 5: *Calibrator of Responsibility and Accountability*™

Rate yourself ON THIS BEST PRACTICE, using the following table. Circle one rating from EACH of the rating columns (Performance and Expectations). The ratings in the **PERFORMANCE** columns should reflect how often the stated behavior **DOES occur** with you. The ratings in the EXPECTATION columns should reflect how often each behavior **SHOULD** occur. Total each column, then add for a grand total for each set of ratings. Graph your responses below.

#	Behavior/Attitude (As it applies to this BP)	Description	Performance Consistently 5	Frequently 4	On Average 3	Occasionally 2	Not At All 1		Expectations Consistently 5	Frequently 4	On Average 3	Occasionally 2	Not At All 1
1	Strategic Plan with Checks and Balances	I execute the organization's strategic plan and use appropriate checks and balances to reach the goals.	5	4	3	2	1	Choose One Rating in Each Column (Performance AND Expectations)	5	4	3	2	1
2	Know Milestone Status	I have my "finger on the pulse" of the organization and know our milestone status.	5	4	3	2	1		5	4	3	2	1
3	Team Members Clear about Responsibilities	Individuals in my team are clear about position responsibilities and how they fit into the organization's direction and deliverables.	5	4	3	2	1		5	4	3	2	1
4	Require Peak Performance/	I require peak performance and support everyone with appropriate resources.	5	4	3	2	1		5	4	3	2	1
5	Feedback and Appropriate Action	I provide regular feedback and coaching, and take action when performance does not meet stated expectations.	5	4	3	2	1		5	4	3	2	1
6	Personal, Organizational	I have clearly defined accountabilities for myself and my organization.	5	4	3	2	1		5	4	3	2	1
7	Action Plan, Provision for Adjustments	I have a clearly developed action plan with benchmarks and milestones, and provisions for making adjustments along the way.	5	4	3	2	1		5	4	3	2	1
8	Urgency in Achievement	I model a sense of urgency both in getting things done and responding to change.	5	4	3	2	1		5	4	3	2	1
9	Alert to Trends, Recalibrates	I am alert to trends that potentially affect results, and re-calibrate action plans where necessary.	5	4	3	2	1		5	4	3	2	1
10	Team Commitment, Appropriate Consequences	I have gained commitment from everyone in my area of responsibility, and have established accountabilities with appropriate consequences and rewards.	5	4	3	2	1		5	4	3	2	1
		COLUMN TOTALS											
		➡ **GRAND TOTAL**											

Completely color in the appropriate boxes for each of the 10 statements above, FOR EACH OF THE TWO CATEGORIES: PERFORMANCE (P) AND EXPECTATION (E), so you create a bar graph to easily spot your highest and lowest ratings). (For example, if you scored "5" on statement #1, color in all five boxes for that number.)

Graph Your Responses to Best Practice 5

BP 5: CALIBRATOR OF RESPONSIBILITY AND ACCOUNTABILITY™																				
Rating	P	E	P	E	P	E	P	E	P	E	P	E	P	E	P	E	P	E	P	E
5-Consistently																				
4-Frequently																				
3-On Average																				
2-Occasionally																				
1-Not at all																				
Statement #	1		2		3		4		5		6		7		8		9		10	

Master Scoring Grid

Transfer the total scores from each Best Practice page.

TOTAL SCORES And LEVELS	Best Practice									
	1 Holder of Vision and Values™		2 Creator of Collaboration and Innovation™		3 Influencer of Inspiration and Leadership™		4 Advocate of Differences and Community™		5 Calibrator of Responsibility and Accountability™	
	P Performance	E Expectation	P Performance	E Expectation	P Performance	E Expectation	P Performance	E Expectation	P Performance	E Expectation
Practice Mastery	☆ 46-50	☆ 46-50	☆ 46-50	☆ 46-50	☆ 46-50	☆ 46-50	☆ 46-50	☆ 46-50	☆ 46-50	☆ 46-50
Practice Proficiency	☐ 40-45	☐ 40-45	☐ 40-45	☐ 40-45	☐ 40-45	☐ 40-45	☐ 40-45	☐ 40-45	☐ 40-45	☐ 40-45
Practice Apprenticeship	○ 25-39	○ 25-39	○ 25-39	○ 25-39	○ 25-39	○ 25-39	○ 25-39	○ 25-39	○ 25-39	○ 25-39
Practice Knowledge	⬡ 16-24	⬡ 16-24	⬡ 16-24	⬡ 16-24	⬡ 16-24	⬡ 16-24	⬡ 16-24	⬡ 16-24	⬡ 16-24	⬡ 16-24
Practice Awareness	△ 10-15	△ 10-15	△ 10-15	△ 10-15	△ 10-15	△ 10-15	△ 10-15	△ 10-15	△ 10-15	△ 10-15

In general, where is your practice competency? Any surprises? Do you need to revisit anything? Where do you go from here?

www.ingramcontent.com/pod-product-compliance
Lightning Source LLC
Chambersburg PA
CBHW050748100426
42744CB00012BA/1929